Mother of Stories

MOTHER of STORIES
an elegy

ALICE DAILEY

FORDHAM UNIVERSITY PRESS

NEW YORK 2024

Copyright © 2024 Fordham University Press

Fordham University Press gratefully acknowledges financial assistance and support provided for the publication of this book by Villanova University.

All rights reserved. No part of this publication may be reproduced, stored in a retrieval system, or transmitted in any form or by any means—electronic, mechanical, photocopy, recording, or any other—except for brief quotations in printed reviews, without the prior permission of the publisher.

Fordham University Press has no responsibility for the persistence or accuracy of URLs for external or third-party Internet websites referred to in this publication and does not guarantee that any content on such websites is, or will remain, accurate or appropriate.

Fordham University Press also publishes its books in a variety of electronic formats. Some content that appears in print may not be available in electronic books.

Visit us online at www.fordhampress.com.

Library of Congress Cataloging-in-Publication Data available online at https://catalog.loc.gov.

Printed in the United States of America
26 25 24   5 4 3 2 1
First edition

Mother of Stories

the word "martyr," from the Greek word μάρτυς, which originally denoted an individual who offered verbal "witness," not someone who actually died.

family emergency

Alice Dailey

Sent: Tuesday, November 7, 2017 at 3:51 PM
To:
Cc: **TOP:Shakespeare:History Plays**

You replied to this message on 11/13/17, 2:37 PM.

Dear Students,

I am writing to let you know that I am flying to California to be with my family. My mother died early yesterday morning after a long illness. I wanted to teach today so as to lose as little class time as possible.

I hope not to miss any more than two class meetings but can't give you a firm schedule at the moment. I will be in touch when the next week becomes clearer. I apologize for the disruption and appreciate your patience.

I was grateful to be able to teach this morning. It made things feel normal for a few hours. Thank you for that.

Best,
AD

OCTOBER

I.

It's Columbus Day weekend. We have driven from Philadelphia to New Bern, North Carolina, to visit my mother-in-law. The drive should take eight hours but has taken thirteen. Before we arrive at her house, we stop at a sparkling new grocery store to buy wine. We used to bring recipes, cooking equipment, and ingredients, but that was when she still lived in Pennsylvania.

We have been there less than twenty-four hours when my sister Joyce begins to call from Portland. By the time I look at my phone, she has called repeatedly, and I know something must be wrong. We have come to a little port village for dinner with my mother-in-law and her husband. I am getting out of the car when I call my sister back. I am standing on the sidewalk when she picks up the phone. The others are walking away from me down the street.

This is what she tells me secondhand from my father and older brother, who live in San Diego with my mom: My mother woke up the day before in some altered state. She's unable to stand. She can't sit upright without collapsing and falling forward. She blanks out in the middle of chewing. My father tied her to an armchair in the living room to keep her from injuring herself while he went out to buy a bedside commode. She refused to use it and instead demanded repeatedly to be taken to the bathroom. My father resisted, saying he couldn't support her weight, but eventually he gave in and tried to help her down the hallway. There, she was seized with another lapse in consciousness and crashed to the floor. Now something is wrong with her ankle. She swore months ago that she never wanted to be hospitalized again, so my father doesn't know what to do.

Joyce can't tell me what could be causing this. She has no way to know. I want her to know because she's a doctor, and we need doctors to name causes and mark off clear parameters for what's to come. Could it be seizures or a stroke? Or a reaction to the narcotics?

"Do I need to come out?" I ask.

"I don't know," she tells me. "Wait until tomorrow. We'll know more then."

The risotto at the restaurant is burnt. My son is tired from a day at the beach and sleeps out dinner in my arms.

The next day, my father phones from the hospital. My mother finally asked him to call 911, but now that an ambulance has delivered her there, she's refusing treatment. Her ankle was shattered in the fall. She needs surgery, if only to return to hospice care at home. She is not eating or drinking.

My sister calls an hour later, crying hard. She has spoken to the ICU physician, and she is leaving her weekend cardiology conference to fly down. If I have any hope of seeing my mother sentient again, I need to come now.

I am hours from a major airport and can't get to San Diego any sooner than late the next morning. I have only three days' clothes with me. No laptop, none of the student papers I planned to grade that week over my fall break, none of the five or six books I need to read. The only store open in New Bern, North Carolina, on the Sunday night of Columbus Day weekend is Walmart. I buy a gray cardigan and a pink hoodie. The next morning, my husband drives me to the smallest airport I've ever seen.

I remember nothing about the flight. These blanks will become a feature of my life.

When I land, my brother Paul is arriving simultaneously only a few gates away on a flight from Syracuse. We take a shuttle to a multistory rental car facility a mile from the airport. The man at the counter is friendly. Maybe we look like tourists. "What brings you to town?" he chirps.

I recognize his question as a test that I will fail—a test I am already failing. A simple ritual between human beings that I cannot now perform.

It will be months before I can answer such questions. I pause at the rental counter in search of a reply, give up, and say, "Our mother is dying."

Alice Dailey and Chelsea Phillips, Villanova University

Performance Script for
"To please to-morrow's audience": Ending *The Spanish Tragedy*"
Friday, October 27, 3:30–4:45pm

[EXCERPT]

KING. Why speak'st thou not?

HIERONIMO.
Never shalt thou force me to reveal
The thing which I have vowed inviolate.
Pleased with their deaths, and eased with their revenge,
First take my tongue, and afterwards my heart.

HIERONIMO bites his tongue off and spits it out.

KING. O monstrous resolution of a wretch!
See, Viceroy, he hath bitten forth his tongue,
Rather than to reveal what we requir'd.

CASTILE. Yet can he write.

HIERONIMO makes signs for a knife to mend his pen.

CASTILE. *[Crossing to HIERONIMO]* O, he would have a knife to mend his pen.
Here, and advise thee that thou write the truth.

HIERONIMO stabs CASTILE and HIMSELF.

KING. What age hath ever heard such monstrous deeds?
My brother, and the whole succeeding hope
That Spain expected after my decease!
[Moving upstage toward exit] Go, dress we all in black, that we may mourn.

VICEROY. *[Crossing to KING]* And let the Portingale don the like
For Balthazar, our son, untimely slain.

[Exit KING and VICEROY, consoling each other. This is followed by a long pause during which nothing happens. CASTILE, HIERONIMO, BEL-IMPERIA, LORENZO, HORATIO, and BALTHAZAR remain dead on stage.]

GHOST. *[From balcony]* And is this the end?

REVENGE. Oh no, there is no end: the end is death and madness.
This hand shall hale their souls to deepest hell,
Where none but Furies, bugs, and tortures dwell.

GHOST. Then, sweet Revenge, do this at my request:
Let me be judge, and doom them to unrest.

REVENGE. Then haste we down to meet thy friends and foes:
To place thy friends in ease, the rest in woes;
For here though death hath end their misery,
I'll there begin their endless tragedy.

[Exit GHOST and REVENGE. After a long, uncomfortable silence of at least one full minute, the stage hand enters and drapes the bodies in plastic sheeting. The bodies remain lying on stage until the conference audience exits the theatre after panel Q&A.]

II.

My mother does not die, and because she doesn't, I assume I'm supposed to go back to life as normal. A week and a half after I return from her hospital bed in San Diego, I leave for an academic conference in Virginia. I had a dream nine months before in which I developed a stage production of Thomas Kyd's influential Elizabethan revenge play, *The Spanish Tragedy*. The play ends in a bizarre, spectacular bloodbath: Seeking revenge for the murder of his son, Hieronimo stages a snuff drama in four languages in which the actors who are pretending to kill one another do so in fact. After revealing that these deaths were not staged but real, Hieronimo declares that he will say no more and bites out his own tongue. Then he stabs another character and himself, leaving a total of six dead bodies on the stage at the end of the play. In the production I dreamt, the actors did not get up to take a curtain call at the end of the performance but lay there while stagehands came out to drape them in plastic. Eventually, the audience got tired of waiting for the resurrection and drifted out of the theater. A colleague and I have proposed to try out a version of my dream at this conference—to enlist a group of actors to play my ending without end.

    The night before our staging session, I'm out having drinks with friends from the conference. Andrew is telling us about his South African safari and the sounds of the savanna at night. I have not been to South Africa but know some of these sounds from my years volunteering at a refuge for big cats. At dawn and dusk, I remark, the lions made a territorial call—a series of deep grunts from the chest that could be heard for several miles. At the refuge I worked for, Tiger Creek, the majestic male in the enclosure at the top of the hill usually began, and the young males in the pride at the bottom answered back.

    I'm standing at the bar drinking a Revolver and telling my colleagues about the uncanniness of this sound, a sound like grief or birthing. I recall an especially urgent instance of it the morning Space Shuttle *Columbia* disintegrated over North America. The noise of the explosion woke us up, I say, and provoked a frantic chorus from the lions. I try to explain what it was like to be lying in bed in an east Texas mobile home surrounded by lions and tigers and hear the blast of some distant explosion followed by lions calling out to each other.

Someone says, "That's not possible. It didn't explode over North America. You can't be remembering that right."

"But it did," I insist, "and it woke us up and woke up the cats. I remember them calling."

Someone says, "You're wrong."

I pull out my phone to look it up to prove that I am right. I want to prove that I remember—that this is something true that happened. I am looking at Wikipedia. I just want a location to prove that I heard this in east Texas, but there is more than I intend to see: a timeline of the catastrophe, minute to minute, second to second. The seconds when it happened—when the people blew up and began to fall from the sky.

I feel unwell. I should not be here. I have to go. "I have to go," I say, and I can't talk now and start to get my coat and pay my bill. I want to be right about what I remember, but this is more than memory can hold. This is what I knew but would not remember. I remember the lions calling.

I have to go.

I make it to the sidewalk before the sob comes up out of me like a heaving of insides onto the street. My friends are urging me back to the hotel. I am crying from the darkest place I know—from a morning sky perforated by human bodies falling to earth, burnt.

"You've had too much to drink," they tell me. "You need to go to bed."

But I'm not drunk. I'm sober and awake, and those people fell from the sky.

III.

Eleven days later, my mother dies.

Re-entry timeline

Columbia was scheduled to land at **9:16 a.m. EST** [Note 1][Note 2]

- 2:30 a.m. EST, February 1, 2003:

- 8:00:

- 8:10:
- 8:15:

- 8:44:09

- 8:48:39

- 8:50:53

- 8:52:00

- 8:53:26

- 8:53:46

- 8:54:24

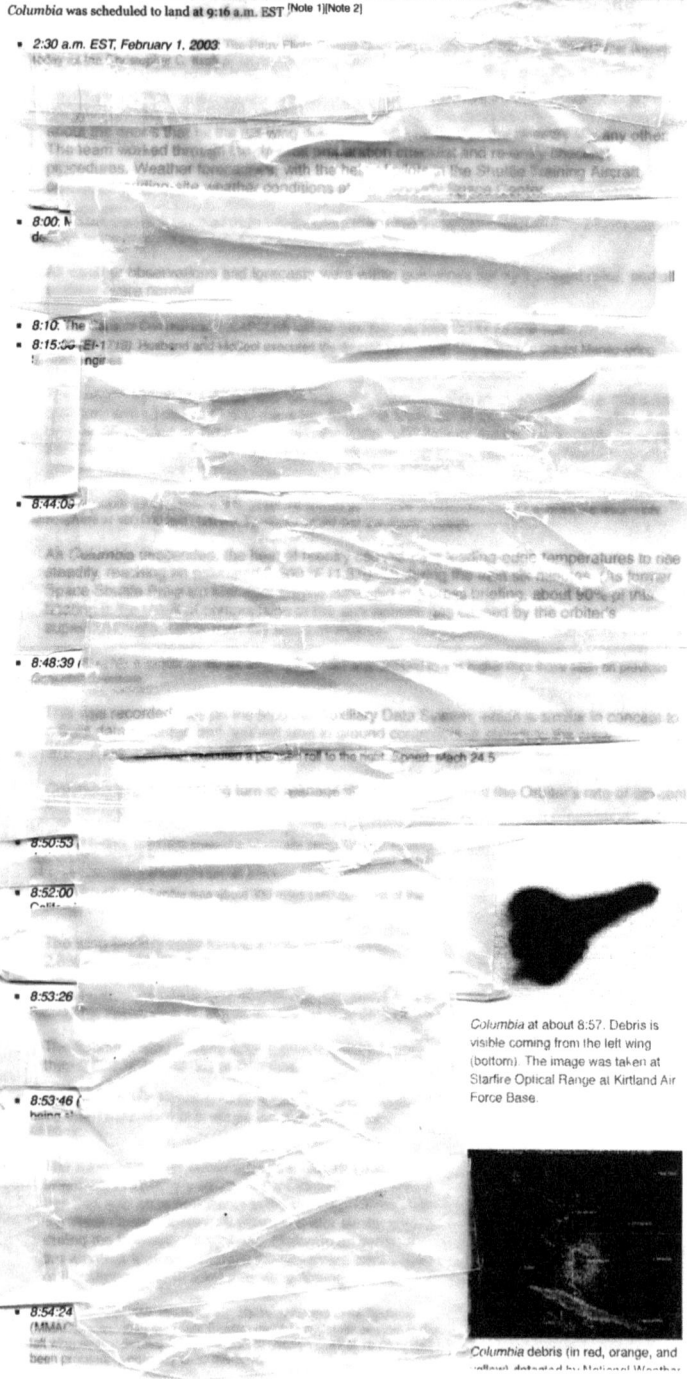

Columbia at about 8:57. Debris is visible coming from the left wing (bottom). The image was taken at Starfire Optical Range at Kirtland Air Force Base.

Columbia debris (in red, orange, and

- 8:54:25
- 8:55:32
- 8:55:52
- 8:56:30
- 8:56:45
- 8:57:24
- 8:58:00
- 8:58:20

- 8:59:15

- 8:59:32
- 8:59:37

- **9:00:18 (EI+969):** Videos and eyewitness reports by observers on the ground in and near Dallas indicated that the Orbiter had disintegrated overhead, continued to break up into smaller pieces, and left multiple ion trails, as it continued eastward. In Mission Control, while the loss of signal was a cause for concern, there was no sign of any serious problem. Before the orbiter broke up at 9:00:18, the *Columbia* cabin pressure was nominal and the crew was capable of conscious actions.[26] Although the crew module remained mostly intact through the breakup, it was damaged enough that it lost pressure at a rate fast enough to incapacitate the crew within seconds,[27] and was completely depressurized no later than 9:00:53.
- **9:00:57 (EI+1008):** The crew module, intact to this point, was seen breaking into small subcomponents. It disappeared from view at 9:01:10. The crew members, if not already dead, were killed no later than this point.
- **9:05:** Residents of north central Texas, particularly near Tyler, reported a loud boom, a small concussion wave, smoke trails and debris in the clear skies above the counties east of Dallas.
- **9:12:39 (EI+1710):** After hearing of reports of the shuttle being seen to break apart, Entry Flight Director LeRoy Cain declared a contingency (events leading to loss of the vehicle) and alerted search-and-rescue teams in the debris area. He called on the Ground Controller to "lock the doors", meaning no one would be permitted to enter or leave until everything needed for investigation of the accident had been secured.[28] Two minutes later, Mission Control put contingency procedures into effect.

Crew survivability aspects

In 2008, NASA released a detailed report on survivability aspects of the *Columbia* reentry. The crew would have had less than a minute between the beginning of orbiter disintegration and depressurization. The structural failure of the left wing set off alarms in the cabin, although they had no way of knowing that the wing had broken apart as the rear of the orbiter could not be seen from the cabin. All evidence indicated that the crew frantically tried to regain control of *Columbia* as it began to spin out of control, but the loss of the left wing caused the orbiter to yaw to the right, exposing its underside to extreme aerodynamic forces and causing total structural disintegration. The crew cabin separated from the rest of the orbiter and rapidly depressurized, which would have killed or incapacitated the astronauts within seconds. Afterwards, the cabin spun around at high RPM, which caused the seat restraints on their upper bodies to fail. They were thus whipped around violently and pummeled by flying and falling objects from the disintegrating cabin, along with their heads and necks being slammed against the helmets, which were not designed to provide any head protection. Even if the cabin had remained structurally intact and reached a lower altitude where air could refill it, the high altitude depressurization would have been fatal to the astronauts unless they received medical attention within 5 minutes, approximately the amount of time it would take between cerebral hypoxia and brain death.

After cabin disintegration, the astronauts' bodies were released into the upper atmosphere and battered by extreme aerodynamic forces and temperatures. The remains of the crew then fell some 200,000 feet to earth, where they were also subjected to burning from aerodynamic heating. The official NASA report omitted some of the more graphic details on the recovery of the remains; however, witnesses reported various gruesome finds such as a human heart and parts of femur bones.[29]

All evidence indicated that crew error was in no way responsible for the disintegration of the orbiter, and they had acted correctly and according to procedure at the first indication of trouble. Although some of the crew were not wearing gloves or helmets during reentry and some were not properly restrained in their seats, doing these things would have added nothing to their survival chances other than perhaps keeping them alive and conscious another 30 or so seconds.[30]

And this is the kingdom you bore me to,
Mother, mother. But no frown of mine
Will betray the company I keep.

IV.

My son is six years old. He loves David Bowie. "If David Bowie is dead," he asks, "is Ziggy Stardust also dead?"

"No," I assure him. "Ziggy Stardust is a character. A character doesn't die the way a person dies."

He wants to be David Bowie for Halloween. We look at a lot of photos, trying to decide which David Bowie he wants to be. When he says he wants to be them all, I explain that there will be other Halloweens and he can be as many Bowies as he wants for as many Halloweens as he wants. "But we have to decide what you want this year's costume to look like."

He wants the lightning bolts. The face paint but then a bodysuit with lightning bolts all over it. I explain that this isn't something Bowie ever wore, and doesn't he want to choose one of the costumes Bowie wore?

"No," he says firmly. "The lightning bolts are David Bowie."

I spend weeks working on this costume. We order a red wig. I buy a white lycra bodysuit, make a stencil, and decorate the bodysuit in carefully painted lightning bolts. I find a pair of knee-high boots and spray-paint them metallic red. My son points out that Ziggy's boots have a black sole. I repaint the red soles black. We experiment with makeup and face paint.

On Halloween, we wake up at dawn so that I can paint his face for the parade at school. We are sitting in the dining room as the sun comes up, and I am putting makeup on my son. He sits very still and holds his head just as I ask him to. About halfway through, he whispers to me in a dreamy voice, "I love it when you do this."

I can't attend his Halloween parade because I have to teach that morning. Another mother from his class sends me photos of my son in the parade. He is looking straight into the camera and holding his guitar with a faint, knowing smile on his face. He has the aura of an otherworldly star—of the boy who fell to earth. I have never seen my child look so alive.

NOVEMBER

I.

She was sixty-nine years old. She died on November 6, 2017, of a rare lung disease called hypersensitivity pneumonitis that is caused by environmental irritants. My parents' house is built into a hillside in the eastern suburbs of San Diego, and a small, unthought-of cellar off the downstairs family room was open to the bedrock, leaving it vulnerable to dampness and mold. After retiring from teaching high school English and history, my mother had set up a quilting studio just outside this cellar. She had been breathing in mold spores for two years. By the time she went to the doctor about her chronic cough, the diagnosis was terminal. Her lungs were crystallizing into scar tissue.

I flew out to San Diego in the spring of 2015, just after the diagnosis. We stayed in a hotel on Shelter Island while people in hazmat suits remediated my parents' house. My mother was now on oxygen, as she would be for the rest of her life.

It was easy to love her then. She slept a lot, and all she seemed to need from me was that I had come. I watched and listened while she slept, trying to form an image of myself as the person I was now, a daughter whose mother was going to die–trying to understand how to be this daughter, what this required, what I was supposed to look like now and talk like now that her breath had become an elemental struggle. The oxygen machine made a soft puffing sound. In those nights I spent next to her in our island room, she moaned painfully in her sleep. Because these sounds were unconscious of me, they felt like the truth.

I made the trip out from Philadelphia every few months for the remaining two and a half years of her life. We tried to talk about literature, about politics, but she gradually became less able to carry a conversation, falling asleep in the middle of sentences because her brain didn't have enough oxygen to keep her awake or straying off into nonsense when the narcotics kicked in. In the end, what my mother could still follow well enough to care about was baseball, and in that last week I spent with her after she fell and broke her ankle, we watched from her hospital room as the Dodgers swept the Diamondbacks to win the

National League Division Series. She had followed the Dodgers all her life. They were her only unselfish love.

As she grew sicker over time, her need for narcotics increased. She began to experience air hunger, a term for the panic pulmonary patients feel when they don't get enough air. Morphine takes the edge off the terror of suffocating to death.

By the time of that final hospitalization, her kidneys weren't metabolizing the morphine at the rate she was taking it in, and she had gone into some kind of delirium that caused seizure-like lapses in consciousness and the fall that broke her ankle. When I arrived at the hospital after my emergency flight from New Bern, she was asleep. Her face had a gray cast to it, and her breathing was stertorous and shallow.

Joyce had spent the night in a chair next to her bed so that my father could go home for some rest. We went to a drugstore to pick out nail polish, and Joyce painted my mother's toenails a shimmery mauve. At the store, we took a selfie wearing giant Halloween masks. My sister is a kissing baby. I am Frankenstein's monster.

At some point on the second day I was there, my mother seemed to fully register my presence. I asked if there was anything I could do for her. "Yes," she said, "read 'To be or not to be.'"

I did as she asked, trying to pass this off as a perfectly ordinary request at such a time and in such a place. But I could not be there in the voice that spoke those words. I read them in a borrowed voice—in a hollow voice formed to empty me from this moment so that I could stand outside it and observe its uncanniness. What I watched was a scene at a woman's deathbed in which my terminally ill mother weighed the will to live against the will to die.

When I finished reading, she said, "It's so beautiful," and fell back to sleep. I stood in silence, marking the irrevocable way in which my mother had just reinvented *Hamlet*.

As the morphine left her system over the next few days, she gradually came back to life. And as she grew more awake, she became harder to be with. She began, as always when she was alert, to demand things from me that I couldn't give her while insisting she had the most minimal of needs. She wanted to enlist me as an ally in her litany of complaints about my father, who cared for her through her illness so that she could remain at home. She wanted me to hear again and without end the stories I had heard all my life of ancient wrongs done to her. She tried to script me into a bedside declaration of the wonders she had done me as a mother, suggesting that my brother Kent had said all the right things yesterday, and couldn't I just follow suit? She asked me, as she always had in ways overt and subtle, to renounce the certainty I lived so that she could sustain the fictions she required. By the time I left her five days later, I, too, was gasping for air.

They put her ankle back together with rods and bolts. She spent two weeks in a skilled nursing facility, came home to the hospital bed my father had set up in the living room, and died quietly a week later in the middle of the night. My father found her in the morning.

To be, or not to be, that is the question:
to suffer
outrageous fortune,
a sea of troubles
end them. To die—to sleep,
by a sleep   we end
heart-ache
That flesh is heir to:
To die, to sleep;
to dream—
what dreams
off   mortal coil.

calamity
For who would bear

The pangs of dispriz'd love,

quietus make
bare   bear,
To   eat   a weary life,
the dread of   death.
un   covere'd country,
No   returns,
bear those ills
fly   her   that we know not
c   c   c   cowards
the   resolution
Is sicklied   pale
it is   he r   eat i urn
n o th   i ng

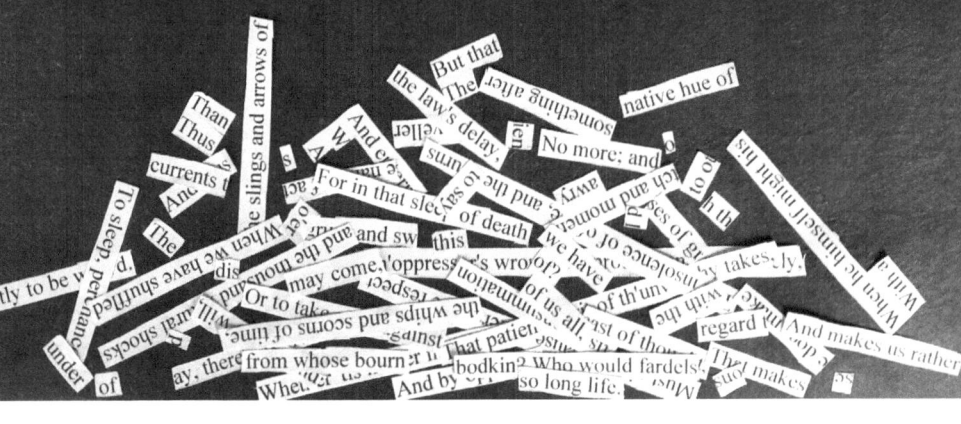

II.

I can't now remember much about my father's phone call beyond his first sentence. He may have told me then how he had found her—that she looked peaceful with no signs of panic or suffering, that she was cool to the touch and had likely died hours before in the very early morning. Or he may have told me these things in one of the several other conversations we had that day and in the days to follow. Over time, he would fill in other details. After her return home from the nursing facility, she had a push-button alarm she could use to summon him from sleep when she needed him. In that week she had been at home, she had rung him several times a night. But not this night. After her last call at around 12 a.m., he had slept soundly.

He emerged from their bedroom in the morning to make coffee and feed the dogs. Usually the clatter of canine breakfast and coffee grinder would awaken her, and she'd call out to him from her bed in the living room. When he didn't hear her this morning, he called to her instead. There was no answer. He finished putting on the coffee and then went out to check on her. He knew as soon as he saw her.

When the coroner arrives later that morning, my father phones me again. He wants to know if I'd like him to take a picture of her before they remove her body. Her wish was for a closed casket; I will not see her again. I say yes.

I never have the heart to ask him for the photo.

III.

Within half an hour, my father has spoken with my mother's sister; my two sisters, Joyce and Vangie; and my older brother, Kent. But we have trouble getting hold of my younger brother, Paul. After several failed attempts, I call his wife. She says he left his phone at home and will be in class until 1:15. He can receive text messages on his laptop, but we don't want him to find out in the middle of class. We decide it's best to let him finish teaching for the day before telling him the news.

As a fellow professor, I envy him these few hours of ignorance. I had already begun preparing for my Tuesday classes when my father called, and now the ground has slid out from under my orderly process, from under my annotated books and careful lecture notes. Paul is living in a suspended past, I think—in an epoch that has already ended. Except he doesn't know it yet.

What I would give to still be in that time, in those hours of mundane oblivion. The irony of that state of being, of course, is that one can't experience it while in it. It can only be apprehended from the future—from a state of knowing how the past will unfold.

Even now, it's not the absence of my mother that makes the world feel so different. It's the end of who I was before she died.

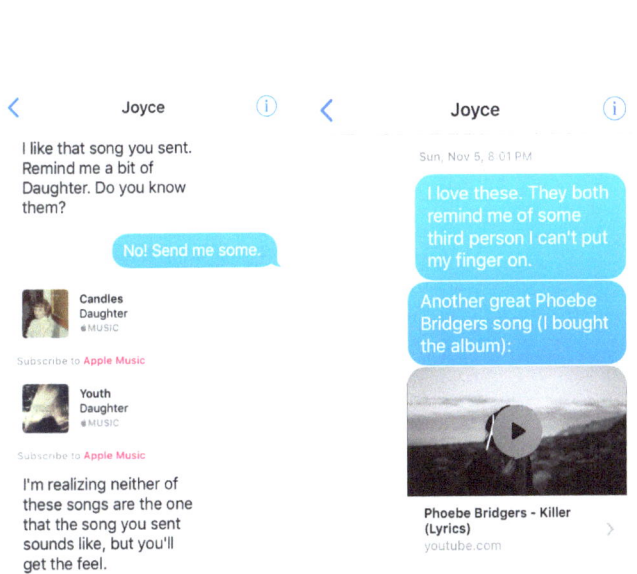

IV.

I am a student of literary deaths. They are my specialty. During the long process of my mother's dying, I am working on an academic book about representations of the dead in Shakespeare's history plays. It is my second scholarly monograph. The first was on martyrology, a literary genre that recounts the trials and executions of people persecuted for their faith. In the sixteenth and seventeenth centuries, my area of study, martyr stories sold better than anything but the Bible.

I have been invited to give a talk on my current work at Case Western Reserve University. This talk is scheduled for the week my mother dies. After my father has called with the news, I have to decide what to do about the talk, which I've been looking forward to and working hard to prepare. For a little while, I entertain the thought of flying to Cleveland to give this talk on Friday—a talk on death. I imagine the scholar who could give this talk the week her own mother has died, and I admire her despite her inhumanity and duplicity. I admire her robotic resolve, her unflappable professionalism, her commitment to the work. Then I recognize—with no small sense of defeat—that I am not this scholar, and I email to cancel the trip.

In the months that follow, as the talk is rescheduled and I continue writing the Shakespeare book, I ask myself many times if I still believe this work, having learned what death is—that it is a cold hole in the cold ground. Can I complete this book? Is it a lie? Here in the wake of my mother's death, I am again asking the question that her propensity to fictionalize made innate: Is this true, or am I making it up?

The question is clarifying. It helps me limn the boundaries of my work, work that is not merely about death but about what we do with the remains of the past and how we reconcile ourselves to history. Shakespeare is wrestling with the dead men he has inherited, and I am wrestling with him—with him and with the patriarchs and matriarchs of Shakespeare criticism who have come before me. I am sifting the stories we create around the decomposing corpse of history.

We cannot accommodate the vacancy that is death, so we make up stories to fill the hole. And then we write stories about the stories. Like this one.

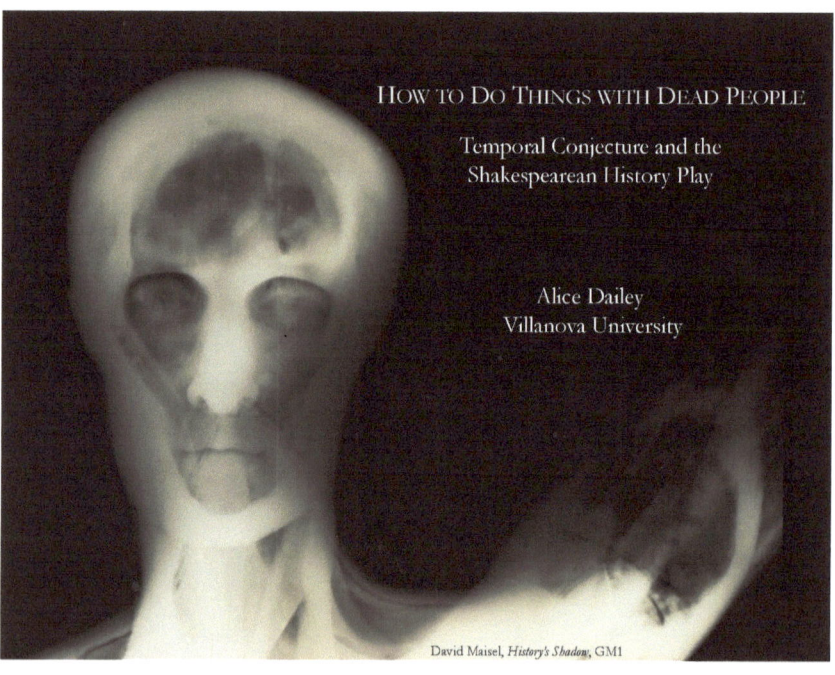

HOW TO DO THINGS WITH DEAD PEOPLE

Temporal Conjecture and the Shakespearean History Play

Alice Dailey
Villanova University

David Maisel, *History's Shadow*, GM1

How to Do Things with Dead People:
Temporal Conjecture and the Shakespearean History Play

If this talk had an epigraph, it would be from Agamben's *Potentialities*: "What shows itself on the threshold between Being and non-Being, between sensible and intelligible, between word and thing, is not the colorless abyss of the Nothing but the luminous spiral of the possible." This is in many ways a thesis of the project I'll be talking about today, which takes an extended pause on that threshold—on the passage from life into death when a human being changes from a who into a what, from a maker of words to an object through which a future of new words can be conceived. While acknowledging that death is a kind of exit or closing, I'm going to be suggesting today that it is also an entrance—a passageway into futurity and possibility.

This project studies the temporal dimensions opened up by death in Shakespeare's English history plays. Because these plays are based on a series of events in English history, albeit at times rather loosely, they have been fertile ground for historicist inquiry, which has usefully situated them in the cultures of medieval and Elizabethan England. Such work has led to the fruitful recovery of political, social, religious, and philosophical contexts for the plays, sometimes noting striking anachronisms in Shakespeare's representations of the medieval past.

V.

Although terminally ill, my mother was discharged from nursing care under no expectation of imminent death. For this reason, the coroner's office requires an exam before releasing her remains. We can't set a date for her funeral until this happens. My father chooses a funeral home and a casket, but no other plans can be made.

To further complicate matters, the cemetery has a two-week backlog for burials. My mother expressly wished to be buried at Miramar National Cemetery, having served as one of a small number of female programmers in the Marine Corps during the Vietnam War. She had joined to be closer to my father, who drew a low draft number and so had enlisted voluntarily in the hopes of being in the air instead of on the ground. He later went on to a long career as an Air Force officer, but their joint service in the Marine Corps was a decisive part of their life together, and my mother wanted to be buried in a national cemetery with the full military honors she had earned.

Under delays from both the medical examiner and the cemetery, we can do nothing but wait. This is emotionally and practically complicated. Substitute teaching at the college level is all but nonexistent; when there's a death in the family or other emergency, we cancel class. I don't feel that I can start doing this until I know when the funeral will be and therefore when I will return. So I teach two classes the day after my mother's death: one on Shakespeare's *Henry IV, Part One*, and one on *The Merchant of Venice*. Monday night, trying to complete my class prep, I sit at my desk crying, angry that this is something I feel I should do. But I don't see how else to proceed. I cannot reasonably leave for California until my mother's body has been released.

I get up the morning after she has died, put on a face and a dress, and stand in front of my students as though it were any other day. I don't know who I am, standing there. I struggle to stay in some semblance of my teaching persona—the performative role the professor inhabits in front of students to facilitate a transfer of knowledge. I am conscious now that this persona might fracture at any moment and leave me uncovered—a naked, grieving woman.

    This doesn't happen. I get through both classes without breaking down or falling dumb or blurting out that my mother is dead, all things I feared I might do. At moments I even become absorbed in the material and feel like myself—as though I, too, can reinhabit the time before her death, if only passingly. When classes are over I rush back to my car, relieved not to have run into anyone I know.

    I sit at the wheel for a long time, letting the privacy of the car close around me. I know as I sit there that however the funeral plans unfold, I cannot do that again.

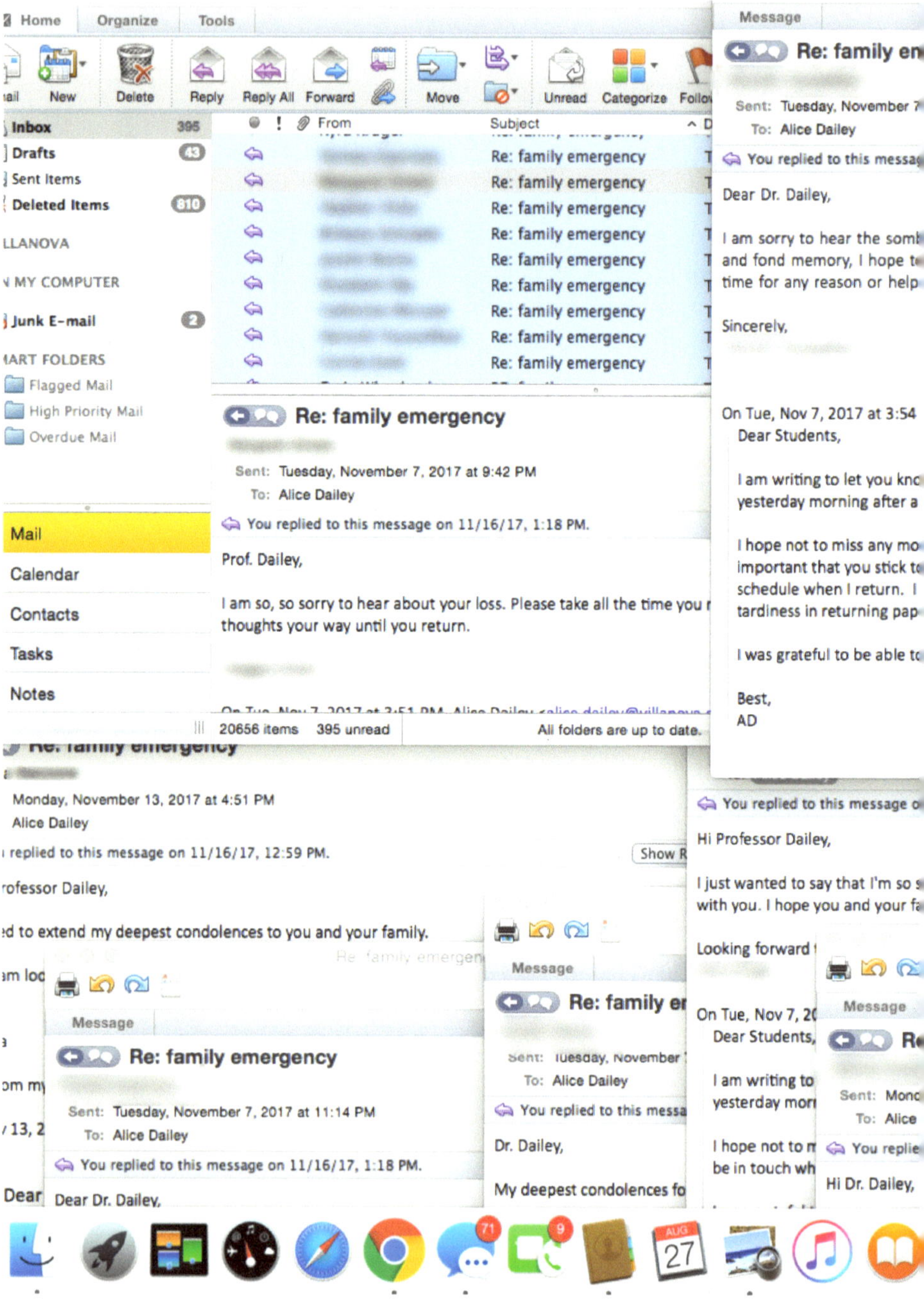

Home Organize Tools

Inbox 395
Drafts 43
Sent Items
Deleted Items 810

VILLANOVA
ON MY COMPUTER
Junk E-mail 2

SMART FOLDERS
Flagged Mail
High Priority Mail
Overdue Mail

Mail
Calendar
Contacts
Tasks
Notes

From | Subject
Re: family emergency
Re: family emergency
Re: family emergency
Re: family emergency
Re: family emergency
Re: family emergency
Re: family emergency
Re: family emergency
Re: family emergency

Re: family emergency

Sent: Tuesday, November 7, 2017 at 9:42 PM
To: Alice Dailey

You replied to this message on 11/16/17, 1:18 PM.

Prof. Dailey,

I am so, so sorry to hear about your loss. Please take all the time you n
thoughts your way until you return.

On Tue, Nov 7, 2017 at 3:51 PM, Alice Dailey <alice.dailey@villanova.e

20656 items   395 unread   All folders are up to date.

Re: family emergency

Monday, November 13, 2017 at 4:51 PM
Alice Dailey

replied to this message on 11/16/17, 12:59 PM.

rofessor Dailey,

ed to extend my deepest condolences to you and your family.

Re: family emergency

Sent: Tuesday, November 7, 2017 at 11:14 PM
To: Alice Dailey

You replied to this message on 11/16/17, 1:18 PM.

Dear Dr. Dailey,

Re: family emergency

Sent: Tuesday, November
To: Alice Dailey
You replied to this messa

Dr. Dailey,

My deepest condolences fo

Re: family en

Sent: Tuesday, November 7
To: Alice Dailey

You replied to this messag

Dear Dr. Dailey,

I am sorry to hear the soml
and fond memory, I hope t
time for any reason or help

Sincerely,

On Tue, Nov 7, 2017 at 3:54
Dear Students,

I am writing to let you kno
yesterday morning after a

I hope not to miss any mo
important that you stick t
schedule when I return. I
tardiness in returning pap

I was grateful to be able to

Best,
AD

You replied to this message o

Hi Professor Dailey,

I just wanted to say that I'm so s
with you. I hope you and your fa

Looking forward

On Tue, Nov 7, 20
Dear Students,

I am writing to
yesterday morr

I hope not to m
be in touch wh

Re:

Sent: Mond
To: Alice

You replie

Hi Dr. Dailey,

PM

.7, 1:21 PM. Show Reply

'our mothers passing. May you celebrate her life with thoughts of joy
:lass whenever you feel is right. Feel free to reach out during this
ust a student of yours but I am happy to help in any way.

ey wrote:

ying to California to be with my family. My mother died early
I wanted to teach today so as to lose as little class time as possible.

lass meetings but can't give you a firm schedule at the moment. It is
schedule for *Geek Love* that's on the syllabus; I'll adjust the discussion
the disruption and appreciate your patience with my absence and my

orning. It made things feel normal for a few hours. Thank you for that.

Message

Re: family emergency

Sent: Tuesday, November 7, 2017 at 8:13 PM
To: Alice Dailey

You replied to this message on 11/16/17, 1:18 PM.

Hi Dr. Dailey,

ust wanted to reach out and say you and your family will

On Tue, Nov 7, 2017 at 3:51 PM, Alice Dailey <alice.dailey

Dear Students,

ly emergency

nber 7, 2017 at 6:08 PM

nessage on 11/16/17,

r about your mother.

Message

Re: family emerg

Sent: Tuesday, November 7, 2017
To: Alice Dailey

You replied to this message on 1

Dear Dr. Dailey,

I am so sorry for your loss. I wish y
thoughts and prayers during this d

Best.

1:17 PM.

you and your family. I hope our class ca

I'm looking forward to seeing you agair

' loss. I th
e to find c

On Nov 7, 2017, at 3:54 PM, Alice Dailey <al

Dear Students,

I am writing to let you know that I ar

emergency

' 13, 2017 at 3:16 PM

sage on 11/16/17, 1:00 PM.

Message

Re: family emergency

Sent: Tuesday, November 7, 2017 at 9:42 PM
To: Alice Dailey

You replied to this message on 11/16/17, 1:18 PM.

Prof. Dailey,

I am so, so sorry to hear about your loss. Please take all the time you need, w

VI.

The coroner's office releases my mother's body the next day, and the cemetery schedules her burial for November 21, two weeks away and two days before Thanksgiving. I can't leave now and stay in California until then. My academic semester will fall apart, and the effort it will take to put it back together when I return is more than I can face. I can attend the funeral, but I will have to miss my mother's burial.

I end up being in San Diego for just under a week. Together, my brothers and sisters and I plan a closed-casket visitation, memorial, and reception for Sunday, November 12. I fly home the following Tuesday and am teaching again by Thursday. I have missed only two days of class.

On November 21, 2017, I am teaching Shakespeare in the suburbs of Philadelphia as my mother's casket is loaded into the hearse that will take her to Miramar National Cemetery. There, she is met by a Marine Corps honor guard and a twenty-one-gun salute. My sister sends me photos after the burial ceremony.

"The uniform," my father says. That's what broke him open. Young men, just as he had been, wearing the uniform he wore the day of their wedding forty-nine years ago. He hadn't counted on the uniform.

For me, it is the hearse.

I cannot choose but weep to think they would lay ~~him~~ i' th' cold ground.
her

ANOTHER TIME

I.

The most formative event of my life occurred eight and a half years before I was born. My mother was fifteen years old when her father, Dr. Kent Gardner Latham of Granada Hills, California, a radiologist, violinist, and veteran, checked himself into the Mission Inn on Sepulveda Boulevard and administered himself a lethal dose of barbiturates. Apart from a postcard he had mailed home saying "No longer able to work," he left behind only instructions for his attorney.

I don't know how young I was when my mother told me this history, but it was early enough that I can't recall a time in my life when I didn't understand myself as the granddaughter of a suicide. I inherited this death the way I inherited my mother's eyes and skin: It was inseparable from my image of myself. It was not simply that my mother told me how my grandfather had methodically killed himself, abandoning her and her eight-year-old sister to my grandmother's mental illness and malice. It was that she could not stop telling me. She rehearsed her ruined family like a compulsion, unshaped by rational purpose or control. Her stories were liturgical. They conferred on me an origin myth that she revisited like going to church. Other kids seemed to have come from regular parents and grandparents, but I had a darker provenance: I had come into life through death—a death I had been born into as surely as my mother was my mother.

I began to openly resist her retellings once my son was born, but even before that, in my twenties and thirties, I had become aware that I was not generating whatever response it was that my mother seemed to need. I had heard it all before, and I didn't know what to say anymore except "You've told me this already," which was not a thing we were allowed to say because it was another form of abandonment. As compulsively as she retold her history, I chilled and hardened against her, begrudging her even the most mechanical expressions of shock or sympathy. I did not know what she wanted from me, but I knew that I was failing her, and I knew when she got sick that I would fail her till she died. I also knew that there was no way to succeed. Her father had chosen death over her, and there was nothing any of us could say to change that.

II.

Kent Gardener Latham was not my only grandfather. I had two others whose histories my mother helped keep alive. My father's father lived until I was nineteen, and I might have liked him if I hadn't been reminded regularly that he had brutally abused most of his fourteen children. I did not hear these stories from my father, though I well knew his struggle against repeating the abuse he had suffered as the second-oldest boy. It was my mother who continued—even into the final months of her life—to recount lurid details of my grandfather's violence.

She rarely did this in front of my father. She told these stories in private with a conspiratorial, gossipy air that made me hate her. Because my father wasn't there to witness, I was suspicious about the source of her particularly salacious details—if they had come from him, if his siblings had related them, or if she had made them up.

My parents came to Philadelphia ten days after my son was born. They had not been in the house an hour when, as I nursed the baby and my father unpacked upstairs, my mother began telling me about how my father's father had abused even the infants. I felt the air putrefying around me. I felt myself absorbing a disease that my child would contract through my breast. Here it was, this history, seeping into my home, poised to infect my baby the way it had infected me: through a breast that was also a mouth. Through a maternal body that gave life and leached it back at once.

I did not want my son to understand himself as I had, as a child of violence and death, and so I nursed him alone upstairs for the rest of my parents' visit. A year later, I finally wrote to my mother and told her I never wanted to hear about my grandfather's abuse again and that if she ever mentioned it to my son it would be the last time she saw him. "Stop telling these stories," I warned. That man is dead. Let his violence die with him. It is none of mine.

She never again spoke about it in front of my son, but she continued to bring it up to me in her hushed, conspiratorial tones. She could not help herself. It was how she knew we were family.

III.

My third grandfather was Jesus Christ. He was beaten up badly, and then he was nailed to a piece of wood and he bled a lot, and then they propped the piece of wood up until he suffocated to death. I was shown pictures of his bleeding body. This body was my fault, because I had inherited violence and death, and someone had to pay for it. At ten years old, I accordingly, dutifully spoke my line with the rest of the Good Friday congregation: "Crucify him."

In the hospital the final time I saw her, my mother asked me what I had told my son about her illness. I answered that he knew she was going to die but that he had not asked what death is.

"You never asked when you were a kid," she said. "You always seemed to know about death. I wonder why that was?"

I stared at her in disbelief and answered flatly, "Jesus was up on the cross."

Day now, night now, at head, side, feet,
They stand their vigil in gowns of stone,
Faces blank as the day I was born,
Their shadows long in the setting sun
That never brightens or goes down.

IV.

I had a recurring dream for many years that began after my Grandma Latham's death. She died of lung cancer when I was seven, and I was given her bedroom furniture. The queen-sized bed, with sliding-panel storage cupboards built into the headboard, felt luxuriously huge for a child my size. But it smelled like my grandmother's house on Yarmouth Avenue—like schnauzers and cigarettes overlaid with potpourri. The furniture arrived empty but for the dresser's scented drawer paper and a few stray perfumed soaps, whose smell thickened into a spectral atmosphere that clung to my room. My sisters and I eventually threw out the paper and soaps, but the smell never went away.

 I would dream that I was floating above this bed, almost attached to the ceiling in one corner of the room, looking down at myself sleeping. Across two of the other corners, spanning the room diagonally, was suspended some kind of tendon or muscle—a cord of tissue that slowly, rhythmically contracted and released over the sleeping girl. She did not feel its contractions. It was I who felt them, but I could do nothing but hold my dread in silence and wait for them to subside.

 Just yesterday I experienced a brief, waking déjà-vu of this dream, a dream I continued to have even after we moved to the Philippines and left my grandmother's furniture in storage on the other side of the world. Although I still recognize the dream the instant its feeling comes over me, I cannot conjure up its effects at will, even if I can picture the suspended muscle. The dream is not an image. It is a tension—a tinny nerve taut and plucked at the heart of me, close to the bone. It's a rhythm of terror that beats in my jaw.

V.

What is wrong with me that I am this way? What is in me that bends toward death? My brothers and sisters lived in these rooms and heard these stories, and none of them has made a career of asking about dead people. My mother was not the same with all of us—she varied her liturgies for her audience. But these narratives shaped me like no one else in our family. Did she do this to me, or is this who I am? Did she doom me to this history; did she bind me to dead men? Or is there some core morbidity in me that has fashioned her into this mother of deaths?

    Is it I who've made these stories?

DECEMBER

I.

I'm not sure which is worse: standing in front of a roomful of college students who don't know my mother has just died or standing in front of a roomful of college students who do.

I had not exactly cast myself as the Invisible Professor before this happened. I have an affinity for dramatic clothes and shoes, and I am unembarrassed to out myself to students as a gushing übergeek for English literature. But I have always thought of myself as a kind of medium–an intermediary between my students and the text. I count myself most successful when I disappear from view. My job is to draw them toward me so that, prism-like, I can refract their gaze toward something they didn't even know they desired: a work of art that will reward their devotions more fully than any grade or teacher.

This love triangle breaks down with my mother's death. My personal life, my family, my grief–in sum, the problems of mortality–are now fundamentally intertwined with my professorial self, and this fact disturbs the delicate *contrapposto* of privacy and disclosure that underwrites my pedagogy. I feel that my students are seeing me every time I stand in front of them–that I cannot become invisible. They know something about me that I do not say out loud: whatever work I may be doing in class, I am also doing the work of mourning.

On the first day I return to teaching, I begin by going through the revisions I've made to each of the course syllabi to adjust for my absences. When I invite questions, a young woman in my sophomore Literature and Writing seminar raises her hand. Her name is Leah. She does not ask a question. She states, "I just want to say that I think you're incredibly courageous for being here."

It is a generous thing to say and courageous in its own way, given how reluctant students can be to venture outside their conventionally dutiful classroom roles. I am grateful to her–to Leah, whose name I will not soon forget. But her comment also makes inescapable something I would have preferred to deny: that my character is open to assessment now in a way it wasn't before my mother died.

In the face of Leah's kind remark and the myriad things, kind or unkind, that my students think but do not say, I am unable to sustain the fantasy that I can direct their eyes to the objects of my choosing. I am there in front of them, and the best I can do is abide their gaze until the end of the semester, when I will retreat from view, close the door behind me, and grieve alone.

John Donne

A Valediction: Forbidding Mourning

As virtuous men pass mildly away,
   And whisper to their souls to go,
Whilst some of their sad friends do say,
   The breath goes now, and some say, no,

So let us melt, and make no noise,
   No tear-floods nor sigh-tempests move;
'Twere profanation of our joys
   To tell the laity our love.

Moving of th' earth brings harms and fears,
   Men reckon what it did and meant,
But trepidation of the spheres,
   Though greater far, is innocent.

Dull sublunary lovers' love
   (Whose soul is sense) cannot admit
Absence, because it doth remove
   Those things which elemented it.

But we, by a love so much refined
   That ourselves know not what it is
Inter-assurèd of the mind,
   Care less eyes, lips, and hands to miss.

Our two souls, therefore, which are one,
   Though I must go, endure not yet
A breach, but an expansion,
   Like gold to airy thinness beat.

If they be two, they are two so
   As stiff twin compasses are two;
Thy soul, the fixed foot, makes no show
   To move, but doth, if th' other do.

And though it in the centre sit,
   Yet when the other far doth roam,
It leans and hearkens after it,
   And grows erect as that comes home.

Such wilt thou be to me, who must
   Like th' other foot obliquely run;
Thy firmness makes my circle just,
   And makes me end where I begun.

II.

I think about the grief of strangers. It weighs on me. I feel hobbled by my loss and can't fathom how other people survive theirs. People who lose children. Whose spouses die in car accidents. Whose brothers or sisters or girlfriends or parents overdose on opioids or pull a gun from a drawer. My mother was very ill, and her quality of life would have diminished yet further the longer she lived. There was mercy in her passing. How do people who suffer unmerciful loss feed themselves or drive a car? How do they put shoes on to walk the dog? How do they live?

I grieve that I have failed these people. I have failed friends whose sorrow upon losing parents I could not get inside of until now. I have failed the colleague whose husband died of a massive heart attack in the middle of the semester. I have failed a whole planet of strangers whose grief I have not wanted to know.

Now I grieve their grief. I grieve a universe of dying. There are weeks when I cry more for the losses I haven't suffered than for the one I have. At times, the memory of my mother's suffocating decline feels like a respite from these other deaths. I am awake to a world of sorrows.

I am mourning your mourning, whoever you are. And I just want to say that I think you're incredibly courageous for being here.

III.

I have assigned Leah's class a book of poems by Gabrielle Calvocoressi, *The Last Time I Saw Amelia Earhart*. The centerpiece of the volume is a cycle of twenty-four poems about the 1944 Hartford circus fire in which 167 people were killed, many of them children.

I am preparing the "Circus Fire" poems the night before we are to begin discussing them, and I'm coming a bit unglued. Why didn't I take this off the syllabus? I could have done it last month when my mother died, but to do it now is to make a thing of it. Could I email the class and tell them to scrap it—that we'll do something else tomorrow? What reason will I give them? That I can't face these poems? That I've been mourning strangers' deaths today and I'd rather not mourn more of them tomorrow?

The thought of further personal disclosure feels worse than poems about smoldering children. I do not email.

But I will have to say something to get us through this class, because I'm asking myself now why we read sad things at all. Why we would read such poems in the wake of another school shooting as news of the massacre in Myanmar is surfacing a month after my mother's death. Why we would read this now instead of reading nothing.

"If you are asking yourself these questions," I say the next morning, "I admit that I'm asking them too. And the only answer I can give you is that we read tragedy because it cultivates empathy—that consciousness of human suffering makes us more human. We read sad books because sadness is part of being alive. Today," I say, "we are reading to be alive."

It isn't much, but it's enough to get me through.

XII. *Graves We Filled Before the Fire*

Some lose children in lonelier ways:
tetanus, hard falls, stubborn fevers

that soak the bedclothes five nights running.
Our two boys went out to skate, broke

through the ice like battleships, came back
to us in canvas bags: curled

fossils held fast in ancient stone,
four hands reaching. Then two

sad beds wide enough for planting
wheat or summer-squash but filled

with boys, a barren crop. Our lives
stripped clean as oxen bones.

GABRIELLE CALVOCORESSI

Circus Fire, 1944

IV.

It is almost mid-December, and I'm still bolting out of class the second it's over, locking myself in my car, and sitting with relief in its solitary cocoon for several minutes before driving away from campus. I cannot face holding office hours. The thought of being pinned behind my desk where random people might stop by for a chat is terrifying.

"How are you?" I imagine them asking.
"Horrible."
Or "How are you?"
"Fine." Except that I'm actually horrible and now also a liar.
"How are you?"
"My mom is dead." < horrible awkwardness >
"How are you?" < I break down crying > < extremely horrible awkwardness >

I make an appointment with a therapist recommended by my employee assistance program. I tell her that I don't want to go to holiday parties. She thinks that's perfectly reasonable. I am relieved. I tell her that my father is coming for Christmas and I'm worried I won't be the daughter he needs.

"Do you ever write for yourself?" she asks. "Writing that isn't for work?"

"No," I reply. "I used to write fiction and poetry, but I stopped in my early twenties. I write literary criticism."

She suggests that I do some writing about what I feel. "You should not concern yourself with things like grammar and punctuation," she says. "Just write what you feel." This reminds me of writing exercises I gave students before I learned how to teach. I decide she's green and useless, and I don't return.

Instead I make an appointment with my hair stylist. I sit in her chair and tell her, matter-of-factly, that my mother has died and I'm not going to pretend anymore that I don't want outrageous hair. There is no logical connection between these things, because my mother could not have cared less about my hair. My stylist seems to understand, though. She takes my already intensely red-dyed hair to a flamboyantly candy-apple red with magenta highlights. I leave looking a little bit new, and this feels good. But it's also fundamentally stupid, and I know it isn't enough. It will not even begin to release what's inside me.

V.

I dream that my mother comes back to visit me but can stay for only an hour. She looks as though she has already died, and she says she feels like it too. She knows that she will die again in an hour, so this is all the time we have. She sits in my living room in a white nightgown like the ghost of Hamlet's father.

I don't know what to do. My Shakespeare class is beginning shortly, and my students know that my mother died last month. How am I to explain that she has come back but can stay only an hour? Should I cancel class again, after having missed a week for her funeral? What will I tell them?

I want to ask her to come back another time when I don't have to teach. Then I could sit and visit with her without being distracted by work. But there is no other time. This is all the time she has.

As the window for canceling class starts to close, I feel a rising panic. I don't know what to do. I begin to wish that she hadn't come back at all.

PRINCE HARRY

This sleep is sound indeed. This is a sleep
That from this golden rigol° hath divorced
So many English kings.—Thy due from me
Is tears and heavy sorrows of the blood,
Which nature, love, and filial tenderness
Shall, O dear father, pay thee plenteously.

2 HENRY IV 4.3

VI.

I'm teaching Shakespeare's octology of English history plays. One semester, eight plays. We have studied the three parts of *Henry VI*, *Richard III*, *Richard II*, and *The First Part of Henry IV*, and we have come to *The Second Part of Henry IV*. It is the most melancholy of all the histories—a play about old age, disease, and death. A representative bit of dialogue:

> SHALLOW Jesu, Jesu, the mad days that I have spent! And to see how many of my old acquaintance are dead.
> SILENCE We shall all follow, cousin.
> SHALLOW Certain, 'tis certain; very sure, very sure. Death, as the Psalmist saith, is certain to all; all shall die. How a good yoke of bullocks at Stamford fair?
> SILENCE By my troth, I was not there.
> SHALLOW Death is certain. Is old Double of your town living yet?
> SILENCE Dead, sir.
> SHALLOW Jesu, Jesu, dead! A drew a good bow; and dead! A shot a fine shoot. John o' Gaunt loved him well, and betted much money on his head. Dead!

I wish we could skip ahead to *Henry V*, but here we are at "all shall die." The central question of the *Henry IV* plays is whether Prince Hal (a.k.a. Harry), who has wasted his royal youth among lowlife friends in Eastcheap taverns, will get it together to be a proper monarch when his father dies. At the center of *2 Henry IV* is a deathbed scene: Hal finds his ailing father asleep but mistakes him for dead and takes the crown from his pillow. When the king awakens, he rails at Hal for his overhasty theft, accusing his son of wishing him dead. With characteristic rhetorical finesse, Hal placates his father and they patch things up, setting up Henry's final monologue before he is taken to another room of the palace to die.

The deathbed scene is about many things, but something particular stands out to me this time. Henry IV's crown was gotten by usurpation and murder—by the overthrow of his predecessor, Richard II. The origin of Henry IV's reign was an act of violence so mythic in its proportions that the plays liken it to the Fall and the story of Cain and Abel. In his dying monologue, King Henry expresses hope that the aftershocks of Richard's murder will end with his death so that Hal can enjoy a reign unmarked by the violence that has preceded him. Henry's reign was tainted by the death of his forebear, but Hal will not inherit this violence. It will go with his father into the grave.

My death is the end of the past, he tells his son. My death unbinds you from the sins of your forebears. My death makes possible the future.

KING HENRY
Come hither, Harry; sit thou by my bed,
And hear, I think, the very latest° counsel
That ever I shall breathe.
[PRINCE HARRY *rises from kneeling and sits by the bed*]
                    God knows, my son,
By what bypaths and indirect crook'd ways
I met this crown; and I myself know well
How troublesome it sat upon my head:
To thee it shall descend with better quiet,
Better opinion,° better confirmation;
For all the soil° of the achievement goes
With me into the earth. It seemed in me
But as an honour snatched with boist'rous hand;
And I had many living to upbraid
My gain of it by their assistances,
Which daily grew to quarrel and to bloodshed,
Wounding supposèd peace. All these bold fears
Thou seest with peril I have answerèd;
For all my reign hath been but as a scene
Acting that argument.° And now my death
Changes the mood, for what in me was purchased,
Falls upon thee in a more fairer sort,
So thou the garland wear'st successively.

2 HENRY IV 4.3

Trouble enough can come
Of this, and still
      I will
Insist on my mistakes

None will say experience.
Helps, but does it –
    A Bit –
I ask for that experience.

No one can tell me yet
Of life and pain
      But rain
Itself will teach me.

I am never young –
Always yet a child
      More wild
And trying it for myself.

          Margaret Latham

ANOTHER TIME

I. Five Kinds of Lies

1. The utterly pointless, completely random lie

Example
We are all at my parents' house for a holiday—probably Thanksgiving, which our family does well, as opposed to Christmas, which leads to adults crying. My brother and I want to make a batch of Chex Mix, a family favorite since our parents' bridge parties in the late '70s. I rummage through their spice cabinet for the seasoned salt but can't find it. I holler out to my mom to ask her where it might be. Her answer: "I don't buy seasoned salt! I've never bought seasoned salt!"

"What are you talking about?" I yell back, incredulous. "We've been making this recipe for thirty years! And what about that baked chicken with olive oil and seasoned salt that we had a million times?"

Instead of simply saying that she's out of seasoned salt, she insists she has never in her life bought seasoned salt. My brother and I exchange a knowing, wearied look. He goes back to the store to buy some.

Problems associated with type 1 lies
See "gaslighting."

2. The appropriation of others' stories or feelings as one's own

Example
My sister's boyfriend's parents have a beautiful collection of leather-bound classics in their living room bookcase. On a visit to his house, my sister takes one off the shelf and opens it. Then she takes down another, and another. The books are so stiff with disuse that they crackle. It seems clear that they're only for show and that she's the first person ever to have opened them. After she has broken up with the boyfriend, she relates this incident one night at the dinner table.

Some months later, my mother retells this story nearly word for word. This time, it is she who opens the books to discover their crackling disuse, and the books' owner is a neighbor she dislikes. In addition to having clearly been appropriated from my sister, this story is incongruous with other reports of said neighbor, a supposed hermit who would have no reason to buy books for show, since no one is invited into his house.

"That's my story," my sister objects. "That happened to me at Mark's house. I told you about it."

"Well, it happened to me too," my mother snipes back.

Problems associated with type 2 lies
There's just no way her claims are true, but the rules that govern events in the regular world do not apply to the world occupied by my mother. Accepting this would make life with her a lot easier.

3. The projection of one's feelings onto other people, inevitably with a demonizing result

Example
My mother has a portable oxygen compressor. It looks a lot like a handbag except that it has a tube coming out of it that blows oxygen into her nose. I suspect she is ashamed of this equipment and of how it renders her ill health visible. But she does not admit to feeling this. Instead, she claims that random strangers make snarky comments to her about how many packs a day she smokes. (My mother never smoked. She would want that to be clear.) "Better cut down," these strangers say, snickering. This happens regularly, per my mother. She lives in a world peopled by assholes who say cruel things to infirm old ladies. Her world is a comic-book universe overrun by villains. There are villains at the grocery store, in a restaurant, or passing by while she struggles out of the car with her walker and handicapped placard.

Problems associated with type 3 lies
Arguing that these events probably aren't happening is received by my mother as reinforcing the affronts by all the villain-assholes. Arguing this makes one a villain-asshole, and none of us wants to be that, especially because my mother is expressing humiliation and shame, possibly even crying as she relates these stories that are unlikely to be true. My mother is in pain. She tells these stories because they communicate something emotionally real for her, even if they are factually false. The only available humane responses are a) leaving one's hearing aid on the nightstand that day, which allows one to occupy a zen-like state of obliviousness to all of this (my father's preferred strategy); or b) siding with her against the world, a tactic that satisfies her but makes one complicit in turning decent people into really bad people. These people may be strangers or distant associates, or they may be members of the family. Father. Sister. Daughter. Son.

4. Historical revisionism

Example
When it's time for me to go to college, my mother thinks I should attend a community college up the road. She doesn't find me especially promising, it seems, and she has always said my older brother is smarter. I disagree, and I apply to a Catholic university a few hours away. I want to go to a Catholic school because I was raised Catholic and identify as Catholic, and I hope being in a Catholic community will be reassuring as I enter the intimidating world of higher education. I am admitted to this university with a small scholarship, and I attend Mass on campus every week for my first two years.

(My faith will not survive college, but that's another story.)

My mother believes I have chosen this university over the community college because I'm a snob who "wants to hang out with rich kids." But she doesn't say this until several years later. In the shorter term, I simply come to understand that I have somehow morphed into a villain-asshole and am more or less on my own. My roommate's mother sends care packages of mundane dry goods inscribed with notes of love and encouragement: boxed mac and cheese, deodorant and tampons, gum, a pair of jammies. My mother calls me in a rage after I have come home for the weekend and not left money for two loads' worth of laundry soap. I am "a selfish user." When I move in with my future husband for the summer after my junior year because I'm broke and working two jobs to save enough to pay senior year's tuition, she revokes the $100 a month she had been sending on the grounds that premarital cohabitation is immoral.

Her hostility—born from a lie whose details elude me to this day (probably type 3)—aggregates over time, ultimately setting the stage for a colossal type 3 lie in which I am cast as a monster who takes pleasure in emotionally abusing young children. The story goes something like this:

> This is not a story to pass on.

When I find out about this after several mysterious snubbings by relatives, I confront my mother. I accuse her of reproducing the demonization and betrayal that marked her mother's treatment of her. She acknowledges this as true and admits that it has been some time since she stopped loving me.

She is deeply contrite, and I forgive her, though I will never again trust her. (Have I forgiven her?) The guilt and shame of all this are so painful for her that she cannot leave it in the past. Some years later, she begins to rationalize this period of our relationship and to ask for my participation in this rationalization. Her withholding of college financial support gradually comes to stand in, metonymically, for the greater shame of her betrayal. I'm at a scholarly conference in Canada and get an email from her in the middle of the night that's at once abject with shame and fraught with rationalizations. This is not the first such email, and I tell her to stop sending them. Then it begins in person or over the phone. "I didn't understand how financial aid worked," she says. "It was different when I was in college." This is beside the point, I think, recalling the laundry soap. But I have no interest in discussing this. What I want is to not be asked to return to these episodes again and again for the rest of her time on earth.

She cannot give me that. She wants the past to have been different than it was, and she wants me to tell her it was different. And it is this persistent demand—not what happened in the past—that strains relations between us in the present. She's asking me now to lie to myself for her—to remember my own life differently than I do.

Problems associated with type 4 lies
I will betray objective reality for her, but I will not betray myself.

5. The simulacrum of honesty

Example
It is the final afternoon I will spend with my mother before her death, though I don't know this at the time. I'm hoping to get through it without her asking the question she has asked on each of my last several visits. Inevitably, she asks. She takes my hand and looks up at me from her hospital bed. "Do you have any beefs with me?"

One way around this question would be to faux-pedantically correct her pluralization of "beefs" to "beeves" and then chuckle the whole thing off. But I don't think of that until after she is dead.

This question simulates a deathbed conversation in which outstanding grudges between the dying and surviving parties are cleared up, such that the dying party does not leave the survivor with unresolved bad feelings—with beeves. I know from my long history with my mother, however, that that's not really the conversation we're having. In this conversation, only a narrow range of answers is being solicited. I could mention that one time when she did a thing that hurt my feelings, or I could say that I wish suchand-such had happened or hadn't happened.

I cannot say what is true for me, which is that her emotional needs have always taken precedence over mine—over everyone's. That her needs are tyrannical—that they have pressed me into calling down "up" and white "black." That my relationship with her is predicated on my dishonesty, and I don't want it to be this way.

Her question does not invite these answers. It demands an encore performance of my dishonesty. Knowing this, I do not disappoint:

"My only beef with you is that you keep asking me this question."

Problems associated with type 5 lies
This is the last time I will hold my mother's hand.

II. Ten Kinds of Truth

1. A drawing of my mother and me sewing, early elementary school

2. Mother's Day card, elementary school

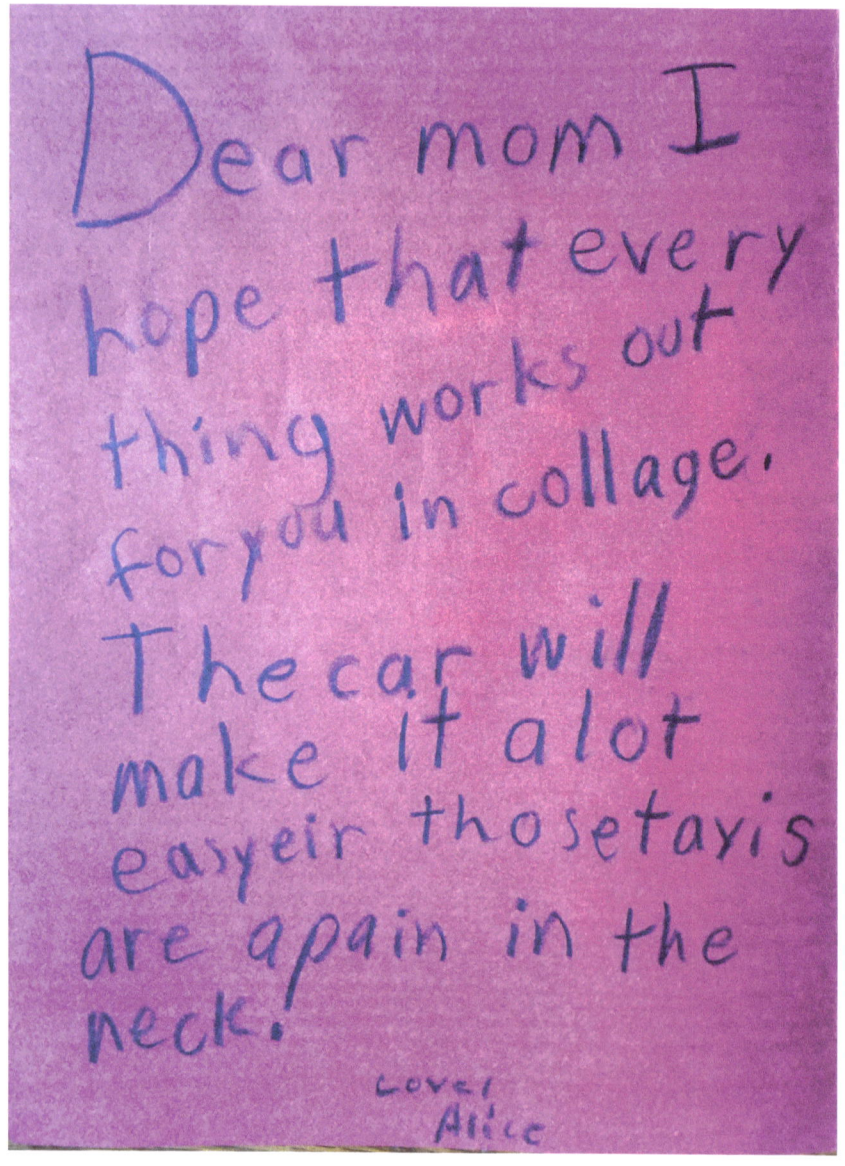

Dear mom I hope that every thing works out for you in collage. The car will make it a lot easyeir those tayis are apain in the neck.

Love,
Alice

3. Thank-you card, June 23, 1988 (summer before senior year of high school)

June 23, 1988

Mommy —

thanks for
bearing with me!

I know it's a pain sometimes because I'm such a spontaneous right-sided creative wierdo. Thank you for bearing with me in all my spontaneity.
You are such a beautiful woman, mommy. You give so much of yourself to us everyday. You love me even though I so often fall short of perfection. I always feel better when I've told you how I feel. Thank you for always being there to listen to my adolescent soap opera. I know it's probably not what you want to do most of the time, & yet you're always happy to listen. You are my most consistent, constant friend. You are my best friend. Thank you. I love you mommy, and no matter where I end up I know your love will always be with me. yours, Alice

4. Reply, June 24, 1988

June 24, 1988

Dear Alice,

    I want you to know that I love your spontaneity. I love seeing you free & not hindered by a lot of crap as I was at your age. I know that in time you will become more disciplined and balanced, but I hope you will stay free.

    Since you were born, all these years, I've wanted you to grow up feeling loved. It seems you do. I'm so grateful to God for that. You just can't even imagine how desolate and desperate I was at your age. I was so needy & really unable to give to anyone. God has given me the ability to care.

    Don't think that listening to you is a drag or a hardship for me. I appreciate your being willing & trusting to share yourself with me. I can't promise that I'll never fail you — only God can promise that — but I love being close to you. I think we are well on our way to the sort of adult friendship that will ensure our being close all our lives. It's a miracle to me, Alice. My mother & I were never able to even start on that.

I know there are tough times for you in many ways. It's hard not to be afraid as you face the future. But know that God loves you so totally & so knowingly! Your Dad & I treasure you & we won't let you founder. We won't move away & leave you an orphan. You will still be cared about in every way that we can.

I feel so glad to have you as my daughter, so proud. Your caring & kindness are so beautiful.

Always,
Mama

5. Juvenilia, 1990 (sophomore year of college)

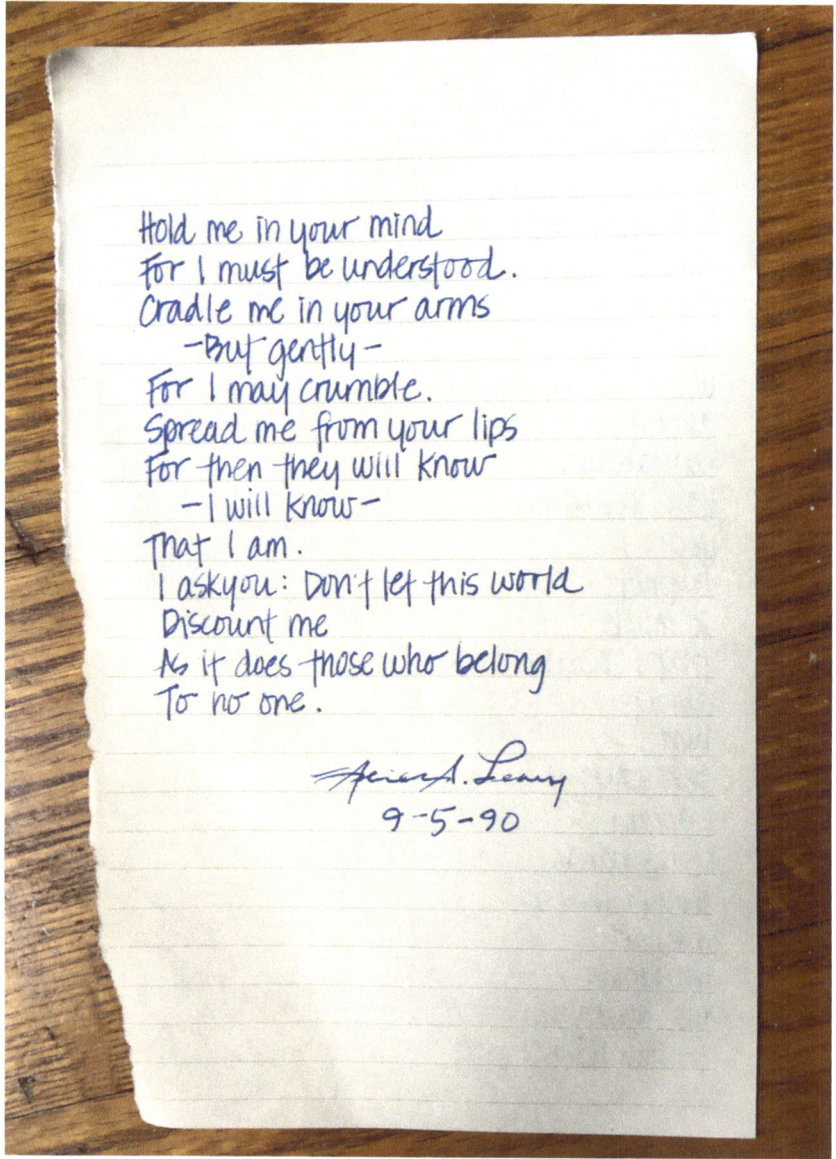

Hold me in your mind
For I must be understood.
Cradle me in your arms
  —But gently—
For I may crumble.
Spread me from your lips
For then they will know
  —I will know—
That I am.
I ask you: Don't let this world
Discount me
As it does those who belong
To no one.

Aiera A. Leary
9-5-90

6. My mother's first full-sized quilt, 2000

7. Satin jockey silks and horse blanket (after Secretariat), handmade by Granny Meg, Halloween 2014

8. Student's Facebook post, November 2017

9. Eulogy, November 2017

Eulogy

Those of you who knew my mother know that she had a prodigious memory. She could whip you at Trivial Pursuit after two gin and tonics and recount the intricacies of the Watergate conspiracy decades after the last book she had read on it. When she was hospitalized several weeks ago, we knew she would probably survive to return home when she casually name-dropped Japanese- American civil rights activist Fred Korematsu in a bedside conversation with Joyce. For my mother, signs of remembering were signs of life.

My mother's memory enriched her life and ours, but I believe the work of remembering was also her greatest burden. She was not merely someone who could remember; she was someone who could not forget. For me, visiting her often felt like time travel in one direction: it inevitably meant returning to conversations, events, and people from the past. She retold long-ago familiar episodes from her life, especially her childhood, as though seeking to banish them in the retelling. My life with her was haunted by ancestral ghosts—by people I had never known or barely remembered: her father, who died when she was 15, and her mother, who did not love her enough. My father loved her deeply; her children and grandchildren loved her; her sister and nephews loved her; her colleagues and students loved her. But she kept a memory of abandonment that she was never fully able leave behind.

That memory lived in her body, and she grew ill. Her heart beat its girlhood sorrow through the far circuitry of her limbs until her woman's body hurt in every joint, every bone. She was 35 years old when she was diagnosed with arthritis. Over the remaining decades of her life, my mother's chronic inflammation built its own neural network of memories, until she lived in a form that could not forget itself. Her pain was lonely, as all pain is. My father is the only person who came close to understanding how much it hurt my mother to be in the world.

But be in the world she did, and she spent her life building a way forward—for her students, for my father, and for us. I want to be a living memory of all that her courageous life taught me to do. To love the sound of the ballpark, as she did. To cook with my nose, as she did. To cherish the companionship of animals, as she did. To splurge on a pedicure. To go to a play. To gather my family around the table, as she did. To have afternoon tea. To make a house of books. To learn, and learn, and learn, as she did. To think independently. To write with integrity. To teach with conviction, as she did. To vote as a woman for the betterment of women. To stand up for myself, as she did. To stand up for my mind, as she did.

Long ago, with unscarred lungs, my mother brought air down from a California sky and gave it to me so that I could live. My mother loved me, and because she loved me, my life is not bound to history. She gave me what I need to live more peacefully than she did. I don't look for her to watch over me now, as we sometimes imagine the dead to do. I wish a greater freedom for her—the freedom of a forgetfulness that she could not find in life.

10. Facebook post, Women's March, 2018

Alice Dailey updated her status.
January 20

Really missing my mom today. She's my feminist hero, first and always.

JANUARY

I.

My father comes out from San Diego for the coldest Christmas we've ever had. We drive to upstate New York to spend New Year's at my brother's house, where the temperature drops to -14°F. There's a certain novelty in the frigid weather, and it feels as if my dad is here for a momentous event. Through the holidays, we carry on a text conversation with my siblings in California about how enviably beautiful it is out there and how obscenely cold it is here.

I didn't know if being with him for Christmas would make us both worse. I feared the grief would multiply with two people to feel it. It isn't worse, though; it's better. Being with him reminds me that we are still a family.

But I need to ask him something that I don't want to ask.

By the time my mother became ill, she had for many years been circling back to her claim of ignorance about student loans and college financial aid. I had done my best not to let these conversations upset me, but I resented having to rehearse that history again and again for her benefit. One afternoon while I was visiting my parents about a year before her death, my mother was talking through some financial arrangements she had begun to make. She turned to my father and casually reminded him that he needed to continue paying on my siblings' student loans after she died.

I was stunned.

I couldn't be hearing what I thought I was hearing. Maybe I was misunderstanding her? I asked to be sure.

"You have been paying on their student loans all this time?"

The answer was yes. Certainly not on all of their loans—only on a fraction of them. But the answer was yes, my parents had assumed responsibility for some of my siblings' loans.

Between a terminal MA and then the PhD, I had been in school for another ten years after I finished college. The $100 a month that had been revoked at the end of my junior year was the last financial support my parents had ever contributed to my education.

I cynically told myself I was not surprised. What surprised me was what happened the next day. My mother sat me down at the kitchen table in front of my father and said that she wanted to leave me a little money in her will as a form of reparations. "I've treated you unfairly," she admitted. "I recognize that."

I responded with gratitude but kept back what I really felt, which came flooding out over the phone when I later called my husband, crying. "I didn't know how much I needed her to say that–how much I needed her to acknowledge it. Honestly, you know? Of her own volition."

In the time since my mother's death, my father has said nothing about the disposition of her will. I do not know how to ask him whether she kept her intention. I delay it through Christmas, so happy to have him with me that I choose not to remember for most of his visit that this is something we should discuss. When the thought comes to me abruptly a few hours after we arrive at my brother's, I inquire off the cuff while I have the courage.

"Oh, I keep meaning to ask you: Mommy said she was going to leave me some money in her will because of the student loan thing. What's the status of that?"

I have caught him completely off guard.

"I don't know anything about that," he answers. "The will she left was written in the '90s. She never changed it."

I am stunned again.

She never changed it.

The will she left was written in the '90s.

I don't know anything about that.

"But she said she wanted to do this. You were there. Don't you remember?"

"No," he says. "I don't."

I am alone on a planet of ice.

II.

Before we exchanged these few words, I had a father who had come to visit me for twelve full days at Christmas, and I felt as though he was with me for the first time in my life. Now I am nobody's daughter.

It's not the money. It's that she acknowledged the truth when she made that promise. With this modest bequest, what had happened to me was no longer subjective—no longer something that I alone held. It had an objective correlative in the material world, in a conversation before a witness in a real house at a table made of wood. The truth would be registered in a paper document: *Alice deserved to have a mother. I am her mother. She is one of my children.*

Some part of me must have feared that this document didn't exist, perhaps because she never mentioned it again. What decimates me instantly—what leaves me mute with pain as the new year breaks—is that my father does not remember. If we were going to suffer losing her, I had thought, at least we would be released from the fictions. Not just from the particular lies she told, banal and consequential, but from the vast, abiding lie that had always organized the life of our family: that my mother was not a deeply scarred person who had problems telling the truth. I had dutifully upheld this lie my entire life. Her lies made all of us liars.

The truth she acknowledged loses its purchase on objective reality when my father does not remember. Her death has not released him from the lie. What I hear in "No, I don't remember" is "I do not remember that you were treated unjustly." *I do not remember that she was a person who told lies—that she lied about you to me, to herself, to others. I don't know anything about that.*

I say nothing. Nothing today, nothing tomorrow or the day after. I repeat my old *Platoon* mantra. It's from the scene where a young soldier has his leg blown off by a grenade and is screaming in savage agony. His superior, the brutal Sergeant Barnes, claps a hand over the man's mouth and hisses, "Shut up. Shut up and take the pain. Take the pain."

And I do.

I have read that mutes like me sometimes imagine making a wound to let the pain out. They picture puncturing their body or slicing it open to release what's inside. Or perhaps they go so far as to make a real cut.

My picture is different. I imagine applying a tourniquet to the limb that hurts. I pull it as tight as I can stand, and when the blood stops flowing, I amputate.

RICHARD OF GLOUCESTER
>   I have no father, I am like no father;
>   I have no mother, I am like no mother;
>   And this word "love," which greybeards call divine,
>   Be resident in those like one another
>   And not in me; I am myself alone.

III.

I dream that my mother rises from the moonlit snow and ascends the steps of my brother's house. She enters in a blast of cold, leaving the door open behind her. It is New Year's Eve. We are all at the dining room table, drinking champagne and playing a card game. Paul is laughing when the chill whispers over us. We know that she has come; we glance her standing in the doorway, expectant. But we don't acknowledge her. We go on playing into the night, pretending she's not there.

IV.

I know that if I don't revisit this conversation with my father before he returns to San Diego, it will become harder for me to turn back from my silent surgery. I am miserable. I want it to be Christmas again, when he was here without the lie between us. I want to believe that we can have a relationship whose principal function is not to prop up an idea of my mother. But maybe that's not possible and if I return to the question, he will say again, *I don't know anything about that.*

His plane leaves in the morning. We are in my living room making small talk. It's getting late, and I have still not decided whether I can say something. I wait for a sign that he can do this with me—that he can talk about who she was. When I finally broach it, it seems he has been waiting too.

I tell him I am devastated. "I am devastated," I tell him. But I am crying before I can say this word.

This is me, this is the shame that is mine

" . . . devastated because she didn't follow through. But even more because you don't remember."

My father answers.

He says that he has been thinking back through it over the weekend and that he does remember. He didn't recall it in the moment, but he insists that he remembers. "I remember, Alice," he pleads.

And my name is the word where his voice becomes the sound of my father crying

"She made another will sometime in the last year. It was never notarized."

my father crying

"I had forgotten about it because I couldn't think of any significant changes she would have been making. But this must have been the change. This was why she wrote a new will. I can't think of any other reason she would have revised it."

He explains that she had become too sick to be taken on errands, and so she had scheduled a notary to come to the house. Later, after he has returned home and gone through my mother's papers, he will add that the appointment with the notary was for the day she died.

"She wanted to do this for you," he insists. "I remember."

My father is crying.

Something about all this is perhaps too tidy, and it strikes me that my father could be making it up, though nothing about that seems like him. Still, he is telling me exactly what I want to hear. It could be a lie. As this possibility occurs to me, I recognize in the same thought that it doesn't matter to me whether it is or isn't true. If he is lying to keep me from hurting, it would be an act of love, and this love is all that I want.

We say a thing we have never said before: that we told the lies my mother needed because we did not want her to kill herself. We told them because we loved her.

We cry together, and he holds my hand. I wipe my nose on the sleeve of my pajamas. A clock ticks inside one of the living room cabinets. I don't want him to leave tomorrow. I want him to stay with us—to live here and be my father.

V.

I am giving a paper next month at the University of Pennsylvania. It's on the new chapter of my Shakespeare book, a chapter about *The Third Part of Henry VI*. I sketched out much of it last summer but have done almost nothing with it since, and I spend the second half of January in a mild panic about the paper.

The play, I'm trying to argue, is preoccupied with glitches in reproduction. Historical narratives, hereditary monarchy, and genetic reproduction are inexact forms of copy-making. This is connected to the book's work on death because in *3 Henry VI*, ideas about what is inherited across generations are often explicitly articulated in death scenes and in descriptions of capital punishment. In keeping with the interdisciplinary bent of the book, the chapter uses philosophical discussions of cloning and Andy Warhol's paintings of the electric chair to think about how death, history-making, and natural and artificial reproduction intersect in the play.

I had intended to work on this throughout the fall, and it's jarring now to revisit notes and drafted paragraphs I wrote last summer. I'm reminded of when I was doing the electric chair research in August. I was fascinated by the literature on Warhol and cloning, but the capital punishment reading was wearying. I felt relieved when summer ended and I could close the book on killing machines.

I struggle to focus. One afternoon I'm searching the internet for a particular painting of the electric chair, and I stumble across a designer handbag (price tag: $1,895.00) featuring a lurid image borrowed from Warhol. I'm horrified that someone would want to carry an electric chair picture on a luxury accessory. Would I have been attracted to—although unable to afford—such a macabre item before everything I read last summer? I hope not, but I can't be sure. That me seems like a different person from a long time ago.

My workdays are spent writing about executions, bastardy, and glitchy children. The rest of the time, I miss my father. I try not to think about Ethel Rosenberg.

x Andy Warhol Foundation Electric Chair Leather Bucket Bag
CALVIN KLEIN 205W39NYC

$1,895.00   Free Shipping

In his cutting-edge collection for Calvin Klein, Raf Simons drew inspiration from Pop Art progenitor Andy Warhol to create looks with a sinister twist.

 Bright Red/ Black

1

Add to Bag

Add to Wish List

Not available for pickup near you.
Check locations

By reproducing a photograph and then painting color over or under that reproduction, Warhol introduces another set of reproductive operations and glitches in addition to those represented by the execution apparatus. More than any other visual art form, the technology of pre-digital photography made possible the replication of an original image the eye perceives in the physical world, replication that testified to the truth of the past and made possible the persistence of that stilled, original moment for future viewers.[19] As in the electric chair's production of time, death, and sovereign transcendence, glitches arise at all stages of the photographic process, compromising its claims to faithful historical representation and temporal instantaneousness. Warhol highlights the deficiency and manipulability of the photographic document in his paintings of the electric chair. He adjusts its context through cropping, exposes gaps in the original by highlighting the graininess of the image, accentuates human mediation in the technological artifact by adding paint, and underscores the fiction of exact repeatability by covering canvases in cloned images that are never precisely the same. Highlighting the potential for error and intervening explicitly in the transmission process, Warhol's *Electric Chairs* expose glitches in our technologies for producing either reliable accounts of the past or stable prototypes for the future.

Underlying Henry's irreconcilable idealization of both artificial and natural reproduction is an untenable distinction between the grown and the made. In her discussion of philosophical debates around cloning, Kelly Oliver, after Derrida, illustrates how the concept of children who are grown or naturally produced from their parents is already underwritten by artificial forms of reproduction, including the culturally-generated notions of father and mother. She writes, "The mother, like the father, is a phantasm, a fiction, always substitutable, always already a supplement for an absent fantastic origin."[28] Cloning and other artificial reproductive technologies, such as artificial insemination, surrogacy, and genetic engineering, raise questions about the ethics of manufacturing children. Oliver argues that such questions elide the degree to which notions of the biological family—the family that is grown, not made—have always hinged on the cultural and even medical construction of roles and relations. In seeking to secure his claim by reference to his progenitor, Henry reveals how the "natural" link between father and son must be continually substantiated through artificial means like the defense of Henry V's conquests in France. Failing to *make* the case, via military success, that he is Henry V's heir, Henry VI finds that his inheritance by birth is insufficient to underwrite his claim.

Calling Henry's disinheritance of his son "degenerate" or "unmanly" ratifies a view of hereditary sovereignty as a work of nature that cannot be disrupted without cataclysmic effects to the orderly, linear unfolding of time itself. If this is the case, however—if in a few words a man can undo the nature of past, present, and future—Henry's actions also disclose the radically contingent, fragile nature of sovereignty as a made thing vulnerable to mechanisms of unmaking. If Henry's legal act of disinheritance exposes the fragility of sovereignty and of linear time, it also confounds the distinction between life and death, showing how, as Derrida observes, "death or nonexistence is already in the heart of the living present."[30]

VI.

After my mother's funeral in November, my father had asked my help deciding what would be carved on her headstone. Inscriptions on national cemetery headstones are governed by very strict parameters: no punctuation marks, a defined number of lines, and a limited number of characters per line, including spaces. The story of a life is then cut into marble, four lines long and fourteen characters across.

It takes almost two months for the headstone to be completed and placed at her grave. My sister Vangie, who visits the cemetery regularly, sends a photo the day it appears. The image makes me proud to be her daughter.

ANOTHER TIME

I.

When my sister Joyce started medical school, she participated in a memorial service that had become a tradition for each year's entering class. Like the students before them, she and her classmates began their medical education by honoring the lives of the people whose cadavers they would spend the term studying.

She was very moved by this ceremony. I remember her calling me from her tiny studio apartment in Westwood to tell me how humbling it had been to acknowledge the gift of those lives and those bodies. She would go on to write a beautiful thesis about how physicians cope with patients' deaths. As she progressed through her residency and fellowship, she developed her own ritual for marking the deaths of the patients she lost, one that she continues to observe. She folds an origami crane for each person and then strings the cranes into garlands that hang in her office.

My doctoral education did not teach me how to mourn the dead. It taught me to write about them in the present tense, as subjects of ever-living texts who breathe again each time we open the book. In my discipline, the dead are never dead. They are literary constructs—characters, not people, even if those characters are drawn from real lives. Thinking about them as people does not help us analyze language, we insist. It doesn't help us understand how stories work, and it is this that we most want to know.

What do we do, then, with the grief we feel for the dead who haunt those stories? For the lives whose deaths make up the books I read to make my living? Where does that grief go?

My scholarly book about martyr literature took ten years to write and publish. That's ten years of my life spent reading and analyzing hundreds of stories about executions and torture, about human bodies dismantled and destroyed. There is no room for grief in this work. There is no room for grief in the dissertation a graduate student writes for the PhD. There is no room for grief in the scholarly lecture she hones to a knifepoint for the chance at a tenure-track job. No room in the first book she publishes to earn tenure. No room in the meticulous analytical discipline that these labors cultivate. No room in front of a conference audience of fellow scholars or a classroom audience of twenty-year-olds. There is no room.

But grief, I learned, accrues anyway, room or no.

II.

In regions of the Philippines, where I lived from late second through fifth grade, a small number of ardent Catholics perform devotional crucifixions on Good Friday. They voluntarily have themselves nailed to a cross, where they hang until they pass out. Then they're taken down and revived, with luck, and are scarred with stigmata for the remainder of their lives, the corporeal testament to their extraordinary act.

I did not read these details on the internet. I read them on the front page of the newspaper that came to our door every day when I was in elementary school. There was a photo of someone nailed to a cross on a street I recognized in Mabalacat, and there was a photo (maybe the same one, maybe a different one) of a procession of bloody self-flagellators following him. A parade of pulp. One year—maybe the same year, maybe different—there was an article about the homemade scourges participants fashioned for this event, illustrated with photos of lacerating objects, like nails and shards of glass, which were attached to the loose ends to draw blood.

For most of my life, I believed that I had seen this in person—it made such an impression on me. I probably saw it only in the paper. But stories, you know. And stories with pictures especially. You might as well have been there.

I wanted to know why. Why people would do that. I understood that they were imitating Christ. But why that way? Why would you do that to yourself? Tear yourself?

I know that I asked this question, and I know that no one had an answer. I know this because twenty years later in Los Angeles, in a doctoral program in English literature, I was still asking it.

III.

In 2012, a group of university archaeologists and moneyed history buffs cut a hole in an English parking lot and dug up the skeleton of Richard III. Following his death at Bosworth Field in 1485—the last English monarch to be killed in battle—King Richard was buried in a cramped grave under the Greyfriars church in nearby Leicester. His skeleton was marked by profound scoliosis and by a sharp, mortal blow to the skull. In the detailed findings they would later release, the University of Leicester archaeology team noted several other wounds, one of them a "postmortem humiliation wound" in the pelvic bone.

The find created a news sensation, and photographs of the skeleton were circulated worldwide. At first, I could not shake the feeling that Ian McKellen had died. He was the first Richard III I had ever seen on stage, and I regularly teach the film adaptation in which he stars. After this hallucination dissolved, I was left with a feeling of loss that took longer to shake off: the loss of Richard III, who had been killed in act 5 every time I revisited Shakespeare's play but who had somehow not been dead until now.

The first semester I taught the history plays after Richard's body had been dug up, I felt an obligation to inform my students about this discovery. To the slide deck of production stills from *Richard III* that I normally showed, I added some press photos of the skeleton. This turned out to be a mistake, one I immediately regretted. My students would rather not have seen these pictures, and I could not take them back. "You know Richard has to die," they said, "but you don't want him to *be* dead. And you definitely don't want to see him like that—naked and broken, wrists bound."

I felt like a fucking pornographer.

IV.

My mother occasionally recalled—with a certain fascinated awe—how obsessed she had been as a child with collecting money to save pagan babies from an eternity in Limbo. These fundraisers were common practice in American Catholic schools in the 1950s and '60s. Children were sent out with small collection boxes to knock on neighbors' doors and gather coins. The coins would then be donated to the church to finance prayers said on behalf of unbaptized dead babies around the world. These babies (born to Muslims, Hindus, sundry heathens, etc.) had inherited original sin and therefore could not go to heaven, but because they had died too young to commit volitional sin, God sent them to Limbo, an in-between place where they were stuck indefinitely but spared the unearned flames of hell.

Although patently racist and lacking any biblical foundation, the "Pagan Babies" program was aimed at teaching Catholic schoolchildren about social justice—about the responsibility they had to help people less fortunate than themselves. My mother recounted how she became fixated on saving pagan babies. In a notebook, she kept a meticulous tally of how much money she raised and, based on a vague calculus she had picked up at school, how many babies she had potentially rescued. She earned prizes when she reached monetary goals: a St. Christopher medal, a scapular of the Virgin and Child.

I wish she had kept this notebook, though it would have broken my heart to see it. I wonder if it would have been as evident reading those tallies as it was hearing this story, decades later, that the child my mother sought to save wasn't an anonymous infant in a faraway land. It was she herself. Her pagan baby narrative was a companion story to one that dated from roughly the same period in which her parents had fallen asleep intoxicated, cigarettes still lit, and awoken to a bed on fire.

A daughter of dysfunction and neglect, my mother was her own pagan baby. The child who lived at the inferno's edge. The child who needed saving from an unmerciful inheritance.

V.

Sometimes when they fought, my father called her a martyr. That's how I learned the word. That or the Eucharistic Prayer—I don't remember which.

VI.

Other than scholars who reviewed the book, my mother is the only one who claimed to have read it all. She found it challenging but interesting, she said.

"What most interested you about it?" I asked.
"Cromwell."
"Ah," I replied, heart sinking. "Which Cromwell?"
"Thomas."

conscience
    and disclosure and transparency,
        225–29, 230–31, 232, 235–36,
        239
    and *Eikon Basilike*, 8–9, 207,
        221–25, 227–28, 243–44, 249
    in Milton, 234–36, 243
Corns, Thomas N., 232, 298n30
Corpus Christi dramas, 36–52
    date, 36
    and Foxe, 80, 85
    and game/*ludus*, 47, 269n23
    and silence of Christ, 11, 14, 28, 39,
        41, 42–45, 85, 144–45
    and threat and containment of
        Christ, 39–42, 46, 133
    tortores and *mali actori*, 37–39, 49
    and transcendence and reversal,
        48–52
    and violence, 46–48, 49, 50–52,
        122
Corthell, Ronald, 105
Cottam, Thomas, 107, 121
Cranmer, Thomas, 78, 90, 94,
    279n47, 280n50
crowd management at executions,
    95–97
Croxton *Play of the Sacrament*, 48–49
crucifixion
    in Corpus Christi dramas, 43–44,
        47–48, 51–52
    as sacrifice, 212–13
    cruelty, 1, 10
    in *Eikon Basilike*, 209, 210, 220
    in Foxe, 66–67, 79–80, 82, 85

Daems, Jim and Nelson, Holly Faith,
    208, 216
Dalby, Robert, 149
David, King, and Charles I, 214–19,
    237
Davidson, Clifford, 42

death
    by burning, 66–77, 91–93, 95–96
    by pressing, 137, 140, 146
    of Christ. *See* crucifixion
    comportment at, 113, 114–15, 117,
        122, 174–75
    as confession, 76
    martyr's desire for, 1–2, 16–20, 35,
        57, 121, 136–38, 143
    of persecutors, 35, 65
    as suicide, 97, 131, 136, 142–44,
        162, 206
Derderian, Hovnan, 246, 248
devil, and persecutors, 34–35, 49
Devlin, Christopher, 200, 289n4,
    295n61
Dillon, Anne, 141, 146, 286nn3, 5,
    287n7
Dionysius, Saint, 21
divinity of Christ, 45, 47, 144–45
Donne, John
    Biathanatos, 142–43
    Pseudo-Martyr, 143
drama, and play, 269n23
Dubrow, Heather, 4
Dudley, Scott, 160–61

Earl, James, 100
education
    in Foxe, 81–82, 133
    in *Golden Legend*, 19–20
Edwards, Francis, 290n11
Eikon Basilike, 3, 249
    authorship, 296n6
    and Catholicism, 233–34
    and conscience, 8–9, 207, 221–25,
        227–28, 243–44
    and disclosure and transparency,
        225–29, 230–31, 232, 235–36,
        239
    and domestic life, 230–31, 232–33,
        234

The legend of Saint Apollonia includes other brutalized bodies, however—bodies that are not resolved through narrative or figurative language into sites of divine revelation. Before introducing Apollonia, the legend describes other Christian victims suffering under Roman persecution:

> Some of them they tore limb from limb, hacking them to pieces. They mutilated the faces of others and put their eyes out with pointed sticks, and threw them out of the city. Still others they led to the idols, pressing them to worship, and when they refused and cursed the idols, they had their feet chained together and were dragged through the city streets, until this brutal, horrid torture reduced their bodies to shreds and tatters. (1.268)

The story then turns abruptly to Apollonia, and nothing more is related about these nameless Christian dead. The legend leaves them luridly hacked to pieces, offering no assurance that they are only temporarily shredded up. Because their bodies remain disarticulated, their sanctity is unarticulated, and they become invisible to Christian iconography. Although one could argue that the nameless dead are sanctified by mere inclusion in *The Golden Legend*, their suffering bodies are altogether absent from visual representation, and images of the communion of saints in the time and space of heaven do not include them.[83]

These faceless dead are recuperated by neither the topoi of saintly incorruptibility nor the mechanisms of classical historiography that organize the rest of the Apollonia legend. They do not get reassembled into units of content but instead remain fractured and therefore inarticulate. Foucault's analysis of the mechanisms of classical historiography uncannily echoes their fate: "For history in its classical form," he writes, "the discontinuous was both

the material and the unthinkable: [...] the material [...] had to be rearranged, reduced, effaced in order to reveal the continuity of events. Discontinuity was the stigma of temporal dislocation that it was the historian's task to remove from history."[84] Although hagiography foregrounds catastrophic violence and corporeal destruction, the hagiographic subject, like the subject of classical history, is constituted through the erasure of that very catastrophe. The legend of Saint Apollonia effaces Apollonia's defacement by naming her in the record of Christian saints pagan violence "could not overcome" (1.269). Unreconstructed by legend, which "rearrange[s], reduce[s], efface[s]" material and temporal discontinuity, the shredded dead remain in the unthinkable, unnameable, unrepresentable rearrangement that is the effect and purpose of violence. They are, as Valentin Groebner hauntingly puts it, "*ungestalt*."[85] These sufferers undergo a double violence, stigmatized by Roman persecution but denied the stigmata imparted by iconography.

VII.

During one of my visits with my mother the year before she died, she announced that she was no longer a Christian. My parents had been Catholic until after I left home, when they switched to Episcopalian. Although my mother had been disgruntled with particular parishes from time to time, I had never known her not to identify as one or the other.

She said she no longer believed any of it. "My mother always told me I was going to hell," she said. "I have lived my whole life in fear of that. But I don't believe it now. It was all bullshit."

"Wow," I said. And I meant it. *Wow.*

This was not an abstraction for a terminally ill woman. This was the crucible.

I asked her how she had come to this conclusion, and her explanation was even more astonishing. She said it had begun with my martyr book. "We were raised to believe that suffering was meaningful," she recalled bitterly, "–that it was something God gave you to purify you or punish you or make you worthy of someplace better than hell. But your book made me see that it's meaningless. It isn't beautiful or pious," she said; "it's bullshit. My suffering has no meaning. It's just suffering. The church tries to call it something else, as though that changes it. It has always been suffering. And once I saw that, the rest of it fell apart. Because what kind of God could want me to suffer?"

My mother, hobbled with arthritis since her midthirties–my mother who limps with hip pain, with knee pain, with ankle pain; my mother whose hands have been gnarled for twenty years, whose mother blamed her for her father's suicide–sits in a chair in a homicidal house that she cannot escape except to die. The oxygen compressor's plastic tubing has caused an abscess in her nose that will never heal. If I listen carefully, I can hear the hum of the air purifier downstairs outside her abandoned quilting room.

What she has described is the buried argument of my book–the argument I was not supposed to write. If my mother is telling the truth, she read it after all. She was the book's best reader.

"I don't believe in heaven or hell anymore," she told me. "And it's such a relief. I'm no longer afraid to die."

She lived out the rest of her life somewhere between atheism and agnosticism. She expressly forbade a religious funeral. We held a memorial in a beautiful hotel ballroom, and I read a love poem by John Donne. Paul played a Debussy prelude. We decorated the room with her quilts.

I don't know how to feel about my work's effect on her. It's a lot for a daughter's book to bear. I believe what she found in it must have been something she was looking for. In our strange way—not the way of faith but of liberation from faith—we had helped my mother die without fear, the martyrs and I.

If God exists, She or It or What or They can't have wanted anything but that.

1956

But the function of martyr literature has always been to reorganize sites of horror into sites of beauty—to reconstitute dismembered, burned, and opened bodies into closed and perfected hermeneutic systems. What Milton's critique fails to admit is the constitutive role of the poetic in all martyrology, a form whose core animating impetus is the aestheticization of atrocity.

In the afterlives of the martyr, we discover a tension that has always resided at the heart of the form: between historical record and typological resonance, between human suffering and human storytelling.

FEBRUARY

I.

The lecture at Case Western that I was supposed to give the week my mother died has been rescheduled for the first Friday in February. My itinerary for the new trip is identical to the original one: I am rebooked on the same flights, will speak at the same place and time, will eat the dinners I was originally scheduled to eat with the people I was originally scheduled to see. The week of the new trip looms like a replica of that first week in November—a rehearsal of what would have been if my father hadn't called.

It's Monday morning. I am driving to work for a meeting. On Thursday, I will fly to Cleveland. I have looked at the November call log in my phone to see what time on that other Monday morning my father called to say he'd found my mother dead. I thought the certainty of this detail would be comforting: it would keep me from wondering all morning if *this* was the time—or no, *this* was the time. I now know the time to the minute. I am thinking about the clock as I drive. In an hour and twelve minutes on that other Monday, he will call me and tell me she is dead. In an hour and eight minutes he will call. I am sitting at a stoplight thinking about the clock when I am rear-ended by another driver.

My first feeling is fear. I'm afraid of what this means. What if I'm doomed to repeat the crises of that week again and again in different forms without ever reaching the escape hatch of my talk in Cleveland—the portal that will take me into a future that doesn't lead again to that phone call? I'm shaking as I get out of the car. The man who hit me is standing in the road.

His face is benevolent. He is looking at me, open, his eyes reaching toward me, his arms faintly reaching too, asking if I'm alright. I don't know what I say. I do not say no. How can I tell him that my mother is gone and my father is going to call on that other Monday but now this has happened instead? I think he knows this already. His face says *I know this already*. The compassionate openness of his face, reaching toward me, asking *are you alright*?

"Do you want to pull over?" he says.

"Yes."

We get back in our cars. Dazed, I cut across several lanes of traffic. We pull onto the shoulder. I turn off the ignition and fumble with the glove compartment. I know that I cannot look at him again that way—face uncovered, uncomposed—or be looked at that way again, lit by the radiant compassion of the stranger who has caused this accident. I gather my insurance and registration, put on my sunglasses, and get back out of the car.

We exchange information. He asks if I'm okay. He apologizes repeatedly. I try to diffuse his guilt by remarking on the oddness of the intersection, the brightness of the sun. We get back in our cars. I drive away.

I watch for him to appear in my rearview mirror, wondering how I will meet his gaze if he pulls up behind or next to me. How could I look at him again and how could I look away. How could I look?

He never appears.

II.

He texts me a few hours later to ask again if I'm okay. "You looked so fragile," he says. "I wanted to hug you." I try to tell him that I'm fine. *The way you looked at me*, I want to say. *The way I have been seen.* He had seen my face—the face I hide every time I step out of my car on campus, every time I stand in front of students or my son. I do not want this man to feel uncomfortable about the face he has seen. So I explain that my mother died recently and I am reliving a version of that week. "It wasn't the accident I was upset about," I tell him. "It was my mom. Please don't feel bad."

He replies that he recently lost his father. "How recently?" I ask.

"In November."

"What November?"

"This past November. Three months ago."

"When in November?"

"November 20th." The day before my mother was buried.

III.

We exchange a handful of text messages every day for the rest of the week. He tells me what song he was listening to in the car when he rear-ended me. I send him a photograph of the Warhols I see at the Cleveland Museum of Art. He sends me a photo from a used bookstore I have been to many times, where he is buying a novel I suggested. We talk about our careers, about places we have lived. We talk about the accident. About how we looked at each other. We do not talk about our marriages or children.

I feel released from the depression that has been hanging over me since my father's return to California. And I feel released from the week of my mother's death—not by the completion of my trip to Cleveland or the successful talk I give there but by the accident. It didn't initiate an alternative week of crisis, as I feared in those moments when I stood looking at the loose bumper of my car. It ushered in an altogether different week and a new person, one who seems to have materialized out of a strange cosmos that has orchestrated this peculiar form of consolation for me.

"I'd like to see you again," he writes while I'm in Cleveland. I ask if he wants to have coffee on Monday after I drop my car off at the body shop. He says yes.

Sunday afternoon, I tell him I am married. I assume he is too, but I'm wrong.

"Do you still want to see me tomorrow?" I ask.

"Yes."

"Do you still want to see me?" he asks.

"Yes."

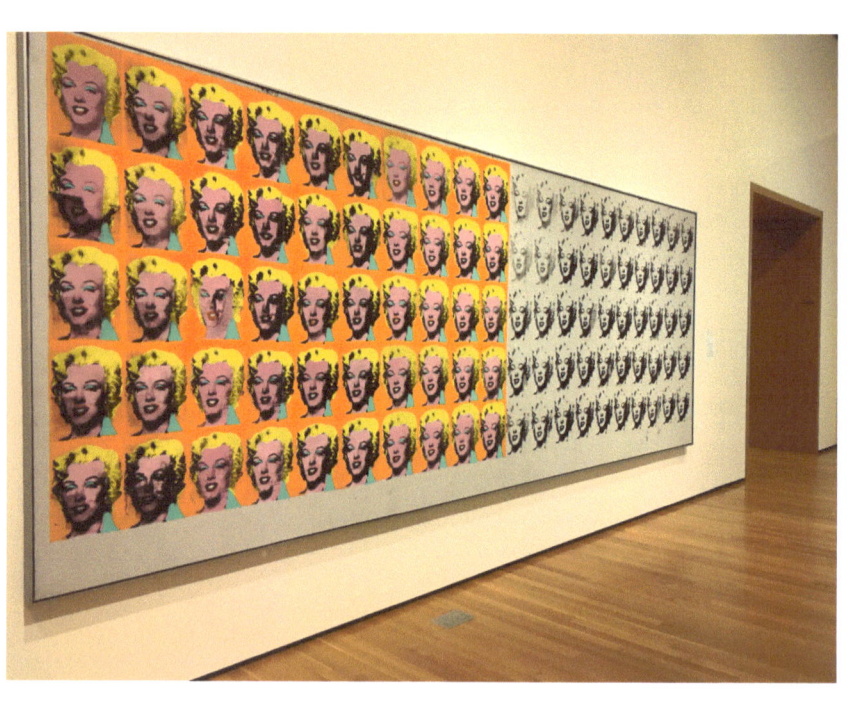

IV.

What do I feel when he appears in the café that Monday, a week after our accident? What are the words for it, the thoughts for it? I am not dead yet. I am alive still, alive here under the gaze of the man who hit my car, who is looking at me again as he did in the middle of the road. "That's the first time I've seen you smile," he says.

"Yes," I reply. *I am alive.*

I am not dead yet. When you look at me I am not yet dead. When I look at you.

We talk for two and a half hours. I order coffee but don't drink it. He has a tattoo on his wrist of an obscure drawing from a novella I happen to be teaching. I touch it with my hand. He gives me his favorite Murakami novel.

When we say goodbye in the parking lot, I know that I should not see him again.

"Farewell, Kafka Tamura," Miss Saeki says. "Go back to where you belong, and live."

"Miss Saeki?" I say.

"Yes?"

"I don't know what it means to live."

She lets me go and looks up at me. She reaches out to touch my lips. "Look at the painting," she says softly. "Keep looking at the painting, just as I did."

And she leaves. She opens the door and, without a backward glance, goes out and shuts the door. I stand at the window and watch her go. She vanishes in the shadow of a building. Hands resting on the sill, I gaze for the longest time at where she disappeared. Maybe she forgot something she wanted to say and will come back. But she never does. All that's left is an absence that's like a hollow space.

The dozing bee wakes up and buzzes around me for a while. Then, as if finally remembering what it should be doing, it flies out of the open window. The sun shines down. I go back to the table and sit down. Her cup is sitting there, with a bit of tea left in it. I leave it where it is, without touching it. The cup looks like a metaphor. A metaphor of memories that, before long, will be lost.

V.

That's when I begin to eat clementines. We buy them occasionally and I have never paid them much attention, but now they seem like the most delicious food I've ever tasted. It starts with a mild craving. I find myself in a meeting at work wishing I had brought clementines. On the way home, I stop at the store and buy a bag. By afternoon of the next day, they're gone.

For weeks I eat little else. Mostly I do not feel hungry, but if I'm hungry, I'm hungry for clementines. Bag after bag bought and consumed. I stuff my purse full of them when I leave for work in the morning and peel and eat them everywhere: in my car, in the middle of a meeting, in class while my students are taking a midterm.

My friend Sondra is worried. She works with people who have eating disorders. "Don't develop an eating disorder," she warns. She asks probing questions about my relationship to the clementines, which I can't explain. We joke about the novel I will write about my car accident with the handsome stranger who invented the story of his father's death. Its title will be *Clementine*, and the cover will feature an erotically charged image of peeled fruit. I send her photos of the little piles of clementine peels I make wherever I am. It becomes a running gag.

By the end of February, I have lost seven pounds. I am seven pounds from an underweight BMI and will continue to drop. I weigh less than I have in my entire adult life. But I am not hungry for other food.

  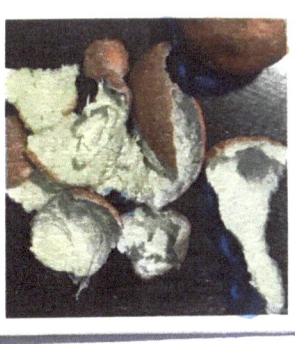
 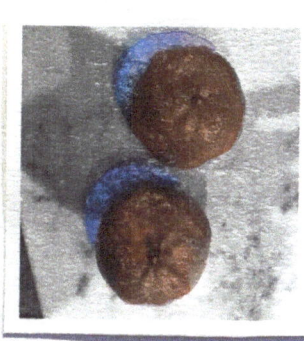 
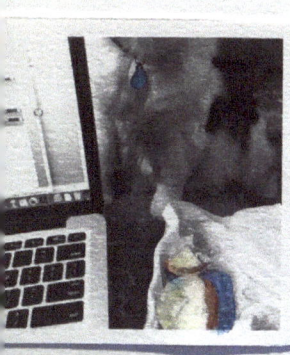 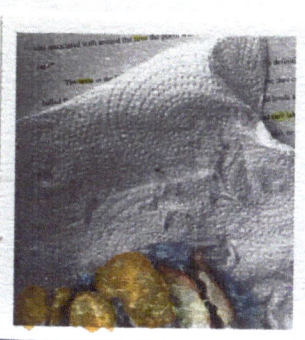 

The Exchange

The economic system of my youth
Taught love was scarce, and money was profuse.
I've worked and worked at love--I've squeezed it dry,
And I've spent for what would never satisfy.

Another part I haven't gotten straight
Is how, or when, or what it's like to wait.
The two half-children 'round me didn't do it:
They hurt and used and hollered to get through it.

Love was always carefully metered out,
A coin exchanged by one who seemed devout,
A coin that I but rarely quite could earn.
I wouldn't give myself up in return.

The system was taught well despite its pain.
The part that didn't know it was my brain.
Of love, and truth, and God, I've often spoken
And thought, but never felt: My heart was broken.

I've tried to patch it up for forty years.
I've built a frail facade of many tiers.
I've stood behind my thoughts and been afraid
To trust someone with nothing to be paid.

I've tried and thought and prayed too much, I know.
I've come to Love at last, and let him go.
He is too sacred to be trapped by unbelief,
And much too beautiful to tie with ancient grief.

Margaret Leary
January 31, 1993

WHAT IN ME IS DARK

1. I was asleep in the bed that was my grandmother's. The bed was haunted. (Are all beds haunted?)
2. I was not asleep.
3. In the morning, a gash in the kitchen wall above the doorway. A cut the shape of a plate she had thrown at his head.
4. This is how a home becomes a wound.
5. I did not like to touch her.
6. Numbers are another kind of lie. There is no order.
7. A four-pound box of See's chocolates. "This was sent by Delia," she told me. "Delia is your father's girlfriend. When we have eaten all the chocolates Delia sent, we will keep the box. It's a good size for storing things."
8. Because of the backlog for burials, she had to be embalmed. She was not embalmed so that we could see her again, only so that she could last it out.
9. She brought the box out every Christmas. It was white with gold lettering. In it were our family's ornaments.
10. I stopped eating because her body made me tell lies.
11. Because her body was in pain, clementines.
12. My cousin and I jumped up and down, laughing, on the old van seat in the garage. My grandfather had said not to. *Goddammit, get off that*, he had said.
13. My mother told me he used to make my father and his brothers stand in the bathtub so that when they bled from being beaten he could turn on the tap and wash it down.
14. "The mother's body is typically the child's first food."
15. I am thin because my mother was fat. He had a girlfriend named Delia.
16. And one named Annie.
17. And Caroline.
18. I made "Caroline" up. I don't remember their names.
19. He left one Christmas and moved into a hotel. Said he couldn't take it anymore, the way we had to pretend. I was relieved that someone had finally said it. I spoke my relief out loud. Then he came back.
20. I did not get to come back. Not ever.

21. After we got caught jumping on the van seat again, I could hear my father's father's heartbeat in my sleep.
22. Once a year, I walk into the Pacific. I swim out past the break, no wetsuit, no fins, and stretch my body into a cross. I feel the planet spin. I am pinned between two elements: the ocean huge beneath me, the sky that begins at my chest and never ends. Each fathomless darkness. I hover at the margin, sensing how everything could slip. A minor disturbance in the electromagnetic field, a glitch in the will is all it would take to come unfixed and drift out to space. Or to let the water take me under, scouring me clean against the bottom.
23. When we got to the funeral home, the casket was open. My brother saw her. "Please close it," he asked. Please.
24. Close it.
25. She never forgave me for understanding why my father wanted to leave.
26. "When you were little," she told me, "you called yourself 'The Alice.'"
27. Each fathomless darkness.
28. The Pacific is my holy fear.
29. I felt if I reached for her that I would never say my own name again.
30. I felt if I reached for her that her father would be my father and her mother my mother.
31. One of the girlfriends had swallowed Drano in high school. The doctors had fashioned her a new esophagus from her own intestine.
32. I try to be perfect so that I won't hurt the way she did. I am trying to be perfect right now, this very second.
33. If her father was my father and her mother my mother, the bed is on fire.
34. Her body wanted to swallow me back up. Reincorporation: to absorb a girl back into a corpse.
35. List three ways that a tourniquet is like a scourge.
36. If she would stop lying, I thought, or if she would stop telling the truth. I didn't know which.
37. If she would stop, she would be less lonely. We would not be wishing for a way to leave her. She has only herself to blame.
38. I wanted to let the ocean take me.
39. List three ways that a drowning is nothing like a crucifixion.

40. She reached out for me. When I reached back, I was a liar.
41. Misogyny is not a mean man. Misogyny is a daughter who starves and does not want to touch you.
42. Let me explain it like this. When I was a child, my mother drowned me in a bathtub full of my father's blood and set my bed on fire. That's why I'm this way. I did not have a regular childhood.
43. I am telling you a story.
44. Cry me a river.
45. When I said I'm not a virgin, she said, "I forgive you."
46. I did not want her to touch me with hands gnarled by loneliness.
47. She did not love me. She only wanted to colonize my mouth.
48. She only wanted me to love her.
49. She only wanted me to live with her. She could not leave, and she did not want to die alone there, in the haunted house of those stories.
50. I let her die alone there.
51. I had to let her die alone there.
52. Cry me an ocean.
53. "Where did she go?" my son asks. "Back into the earth," I tell him. "Will she become a tree?" he asks. "Yes." "Will she become a dolphin?" "Yes."
54. Now I can feel all my bones. My mother grows thin in her coffin.
55. She left us instead.

my feminist hero

                              our lives like barns
With both doors blown open: you could see straight
Through.

MARCH

I.

On the evening of March 2nd, in the middle of a nor'easter, a huge beech tree in our neighbor's yard comes uprooted in the wind and falls and hits our house. My husband is asleep in our bed only feet away from where the main trunk strikes the corner of the house. An hour later, a tree comes down in another neighbor's yard, taking the power lines with it. We are without electricity for five days.

    The storm leaves my son and me stranded at a friend's, where we stay the night. My husband sends a photo of our house from across the street, but it is dark and snowing and hard to make out the scale of the damage. I lie awake that night thinking about what we will find when we return home in the morning. It is nothing I could have imagined.

    It looks like a scene from a tornado movie. The beech tree has leveled the smaller hawthorn tree in its path and sheared off one side of our giant Norway spruce before landing in our front yard. Branch and roof debris stretches across the snow sixty or seventy feet from the trunk of the fallen tree. My husband's car is pinned at the back of our driveway. There are branches sticking out of our roof, and at the corner where the tree hit the house, the attic is open to the air.

    The house has already become a local spectacle, gawkers driving by at a few miles an hour to ogle our wreckage. I ogle too, standing by the curb. My chest feels hard; I can't get the air in. I want to cry but not in front of these people. I go into the house, where my husband has started a fire to keep the dog and cats from freezing. I am looking for a place to hide—a closet or a cupboard or a drainpipe or crevice between the floorboards where I can shrink and cry this out of me unseen. I go upstairs to our room. Centered on the wall facing the bedroom doorway is our bed—the bed where my husband sleeps on the left, where my husband fell asleep last night during the storm. The plaster walls and ceiling on his side of the room are riven with deep cracks. The corner of his closet has separated; where the front and side walls of the house join, light streams through. His clothes and shoes are strewn with plaster. There are holes in his closet ceiling.

I go into our bathroom and close the door. This room is not small enough. I am not safe here. But I come apart anyway.

II.

I took my son to the mall once when he was thirteen months old. I would not remember this but for what followed, which no one will ever convince me wasn't a consequence of the mall. A few days later, I noticed a tiny bump on his hip that looked like an ant bite. Over the next twelve hours, the area around it grew red, as if it were becoming infected. Neosporin and Benadryl cream didn't help. I took him to the doctor, who put him on Amoxicillin, but the red area continued to expand. The fever started late that night. By the next morning, we were in the emergency room at Children's Hospital.

My son was admitted with methicillin-resistant *Staphylococcus aureus*, or MRSA. At the time he got sick, the American mortality rate for infants with MRSA was 25 percent. It took an excruciatingly long time—forty-eight hours from when he was admitted—before we saw any clear response to the new antibiotic they hoped would bring the infection under control. I remember sitting on the edge of the tub in his hospital bathroom during this time of waiting, sobbing into the phone that I did not want my baby to die. My father on the other end of the line, who had spent a career in nursing, withheld his growing fear that this could happen.

For nights, I slept curled around my son in his hospital crib. When my husband came to stand vigil, I left the room for food. Outside my son's room, I entered a universe peopled by seriously ill children and their families. I went up and down elevators among children without hair, among emaciated children and children on gurneys connected to tubes and monitors. I watched a clown in the lobby perform tricks for an audience of hospitalized elementary-school invalids. I moved among the parents of these kids, many of whom must have not only feared but known their children would die. In the flash of time it had taken my son to get sick, we had been dislocated from our everyday life of work and home to this parallel world inhabited by the living ghosts of children, parents, families. For a short time, our family was one of them.

We were lucky. Our son got better, and we were released from this shadow life back into our real one. On the morning they told us he would be discharged, I returned home briefly for the first time since he had been hospitalized. After a week suspended in that twilight world between life and death, it felt strange to drive a car, to pay attention to traffic signals. The world hummed on, insensible.

When I pulled into our driveway, I was stopped short by the sight of my son's toys on the side patio. He had just begun to walk, and he had left a bright red push toy—a pickup truck he was using as a wagon—outside where he had last been playing. It pierced me, this truck. The lacerating sight of it. How could we have survived this truck if we had lost our child? How could we have come back to this house without him—this house cluttered with the objects of his living? This is a thing that happens to people. This is how a home becomes a wound. How the air in a house turns to glass in your lungs.

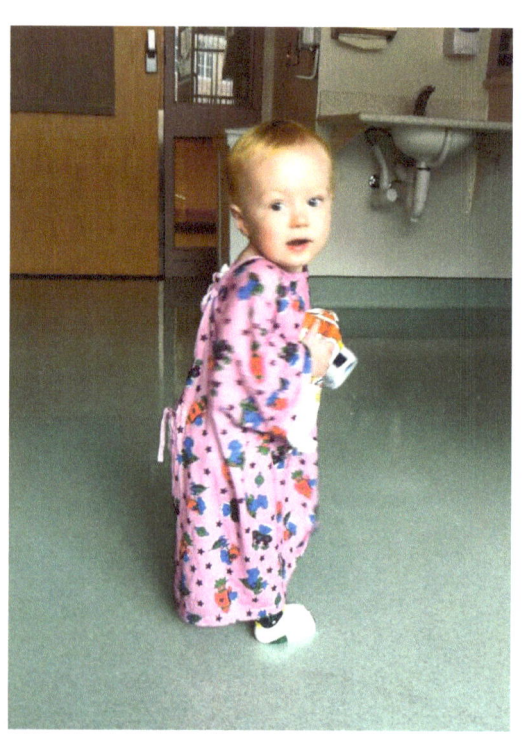

III.

This is the thought I have again on the bathroom floor with my hands at my chest. My husband was in our bed. If the tree had fallen a few feet to the right, our bed is the end of his life and mine, and this home is a wound where my love has been crushed. Where my child loses his father and we are another family of ruins. A few feet to the right and this life, this now, is one to which my boy and I can never return.

The thing about a tree falling on your house is that there finally aren't any metaphors to make from it. It's beyond metaphor. And life without metaphor is the essence of grief.

Terminal
Diagnosis

IV.

I dream that my mother is in the hospital and is not allowed to come home until the government has prepared our house. By law, someone declared terminally ill is no longer allowed to sleep indoors with the rest of the family. Men with hard hats and backhoes appear at my parents' home and begin tearing up the backyard. They dig a hole about three feet deep in the shape of a grave but big enough for a hospital bed. Then they bring my mother's bed outside and drop it into the hole, frame and all. She is to sleep there until she dies.

    We stand in the yard pleading with them not to start digging. We know that if they make the hole it will be irrevocable: she will never be able to return to life inside the house. But the men won't look at us. They work efficiently with faces turned. Then they retreat and the backhoes drive away, leaving piles of raw dirt in the yard. We weep together at the edge of the hole.

V.

After the tree falls we are vagabonds for a week, showering at one friend's house, doing laundry at another's, sleeping at a third's. More snow comes. We worry that our house will be pillaged in our absence: it is pitch-dark and manifestly abandoned. I have promised an editor I'll send revisions to an essay on *Richard II* that I'm trying to place in a prestigious journal. Somehow I manage to complete this writing at a strange desk in a colleague's house. The work is a relief even if it, too, is about death. No one pillages our empty house. We get the holes tarped over, and we return home when the electricity has been restored.

But something in me breaks in those days of exile. I can't hold my own story in me anymore. I can't carry on or carry it as I have. My work can't carry it. There is too much undead dying in it, too much ungrieved grief. I am buried alive in unsaid words, suffocating on them, the gag in my mouth, the tombstone in my mouth still keeping me

from saying them

first take my tongue.

I see another therapist. I give him a plot summary: my mother and my father and the car accident and the tree. He marvels, "It's like a novel. Your story is like a novel. Or a poem. What has happened to you," he says, "is like something in a book." I write him a check and tell him I will call to make a follow-up appointment. As I say it, I know that I am lying.

He's right: It's like a book. A book of stories that I don't want to bear back to this therapist next week or any week after that. I want to set them down.

I go home. *I wipe my nose and the clock ticks like a fucking pornographer*

In the afterlives of the martyr
In the afterlives of the martyr on the threshold between

I go home and disgorge the stone. The words rush out *what in me is
   dark When you were little*

you called yourself "The Alice."

I begin to write them down. *I am
telling you a story.
I am not dead*

yet.

I am telling you a story *unthinkable
had to be rearranged, reduced, effaced in order to reveal the continuity
To be or not so mythic an act of violence*   *advise thee
that thou write the truth.*

I begin.   *Cry me a galaxy, those people fell*   begin
In the beginning
an anonymous infant attached to the loose ends

I begin   *Why would you do that to yourself?*
                                                                                grief, I learned.
*life without metaphor nonexistence
is already in the heart I dream the temperature
drops I have failed a whole planet.
the luminous spiral, a twenty-one-gun
8:59:37   9:00:18*

Is Ziggy Stardust also dead?

Shut up. Shut up and take
a tinny nerve a rhythm of terror a naked, grieving
A four-pound box   to absorb a girl
Goddammit.

I am never young   *the ground has slid out*

he phones me   I love it when you

It's the end of March. *It's the end of March She never changed it*
By the first of June, when the words are finished, I will have lost the sum of sixteen pounds.

Misogyny is a daughter.

I begin to write.
And I return to California for the first time since my mother died.

ANOTHER TIME

ANOTHER TIME

I.

My father's mother died in 2015 at the age of ninety. She left behind envelopes of carefully sorted photos for each of her fourteen children. Most of these photos I had never seen before.

Among those in my father's envelope was his 1954 kindergarten class picture from Lorne Street School in Northridge, California. My father is in the top row, second from the left, with the white collar. He bears a clear resemblance to his many siblings, and the outlines of his adult face are already taking shape.

I am riveted by this photograph, though it's not my father who fascinates me. He is part of what Roland Barthes calls the *studium* of the photo—the general interest that a photo of children from another era carries. The *punctum* of this photo—the element in it that pierces me—is the boy in the center of the front row.

I make a digital copy of the image so that I can look more closely at this boy. He's wearing hand-me-down clothes, maybe from an older brother or cousin. His too-big jeans are bunched at the waist under the belt that holds them up, and they're rolled up a couple of inches at the bottom. These jeans are for a boy at least a year or two older. The shoes look too big for his height and too big compared to the other kids' shoes. And his shirt, also for a larger boy, is tucked into his underwear, its waistband visible above the cinched-up belt.

I ask my father if he remembers this boy. He doesn't, of course, but he takes a look and gives me a quick sketch: "Farm boy. Poor."

This is what the child's clothes say. There's something else, though—something about his face that makes my heart hurt. A premature oldness. A toughness, a hardening. He's a boy out of Steinbeck or Faulkner—a young Tom Joad or Vardaman Bundren a few years on, already stiffening into Jewel's wooden Indian.

I want to know this boy's story. I want to find out who he was and how his life took shape. A poor boy, a farm boy. No college draft deferral for this boy.

I want to reach into the photo and take him by the hand. Lead him out of it into a full-color world where I can buy him clothes that fit and teach him how to tuck in his shirt. Where I can make a soft place that makes safe the softening of that face. I want him to be a boy, not the man he is too young becoming. Not an old man. Not a man who has died or will die. My boy.

II.

I'm complaining to a friend about an onerous piece of scholarly writing that I've been putting off. She asks me what I would write if I could write about anything, and I reply without hesitation: a book about the boy in the photo. This conversation leads me back to his face, and I return to it again, as I have many times since I first found it in the envelope my grandmother left.

The resemblance had never occurred to me before, but now I'm startled by it. The image reminds me of another I have seen countless times—a framed photo hanging on the wall of my parents' dining room. It is of a dirt-poor farm boy in clothes too big, in shoes first worn by my Uncle John.

It's a photo of my father.

sical body of information: rebellion, Nicaragua, and all the signs of both: wretched un-uniformed soldiers, ruined streets, corpses, grief, the sun, and the heavy-lidded Indian eyes. Thousands of photographs consist of this field, and in these photographs I can, of course, take a kind of general interest, one that is even stirred sometimes, but in regard to them my emotion requires the rational intermediary of an ethical and political culture. What I feel about these photographs derives from an *average* affect, almost from a certain training. I did not know a French word which might account for this kind of human interest, but I believe this word exists in Latin: it is *studium*, which doesn't mean, at least not immediately, "study," but application to a thing, taste for someone, a kind of general, enthusiastic commitment, of course, but without special acuity. It is by *studium* that I am interested in so many photographs, whether I receive them as political testimony or enjoy them as good historical scenes: for it is culturally (this connotation is present in *studium*) that I participate in the figures, the faces, the gestures, the settings, the actions.

The second element will break (or punctuate) the *studium*. This time it is not I who seek it out (as I invest the field of the *studium* with my sovereign consciousness), it is this element which rises from the scene, shoots out of it like an arrow, and pierces me. A Latin word exists to designate this wound, this prick, this mark made by a pointed instrument: the word suits me all the better in that it also refers to the notion of punctuation, and because the photographs I am speaking of are in effect punc-

tuated, sometimes even speckled with these sensitive points; precisely, these marks, these wounds are so many *points*. This second element which will disturb the *studium* I shall therefore call *punctum*; for *punctum* is also: sting, speck, cut, little hole—and also a cast of the dice. A photograph's *punctum* is that accident which pricks me (but also bruises me, is poignant to me).

Having thus distinguished two themes in Photography (for in general the photographs I liked were constructed in the manner of a classical sonata), I could occupy myself with one after the other.

11 Many photographs are, alas, inert under my gaze. But even among those which have some existence in my eyes, most provoke only a general and, so to speak, *polite* interest: they have no *punctum* in them: they please or displease me without pricking me: they are invested with no more than *studium*. The *studium* is that very wide field of unconcerned desire, of various interest, of inconsequential taste: *I like / I don't like*. The *studium* is of the order of *liking*, not of *loving*; it mobilizes a half desire, a demi-volition; it is the same sort of vague, slippery, irresponsible interest one takes in the people, the entertainments, the books, the clothes one finds "all right."

To recognize the *studium* is inevitably to encounter the photographer's intentions, to enter into harmony with this field and which I called the *punctum*. I now know that there exists another *punctum* (another "stigmatum") than the "detail." This new *punctum*, which is no longer of form but of intensity, is Time, the lacerating emphasis of the *noeme* ("*that-has-been*"), its pure representation.

In 1865, young Lewis Payne tried to assassinate Secretary of State W. H. Seward. Alexander Gardner photographed him in his cell, where he was waiting to be hanged. The photograph is handsome, as is the boy: that is the *studium*. But the *punctum* is: *he is going to die*. I read at the same time: *This will be* and *this has been*; I observe with horror an anterior future of which death is the stake. By giving me the absolute past of the pose (aorist), the photograph tells me death in the future. What *pricks* me is the discovery of this equivalence. In front of the photograph of my mother as a child, I tell myself: she is going to die: I shudder, like Winnicott's psychotic patient, *over a catastrophe which has already occurred*. Whether or not the subject is already dead, every photograph is this catastrophe.

This *punctum*, more or less blurred beneath the abundance and the disparity of contemporary photographs, is vividly legible in historical photographs: there is always a defeat of Time in them: *that is dead and that is going to die*. These two little girls looking at a primitive airplane above their village (they are dressed like my mother as a child, they are playing with hoops)—how alive they are! They have their whole lives before them; but also they are dead (today), they are then *already* dead (yesterday). At the limit, there is no need to represent a body in order for me to experience this vertigo of time defeated. In 1850, August Salzmann photographed, near Jerusalem, the road to Beith-Lehem (as it was spelled at the time): nothing but stony ground, olive trees; but three tenses dizzy my consciousness: my present, the time of Jesus, and that of the photographer, all this under the instance of "reality"—and no longer through the elaborations of the text, whether fictional or poetic, which itself is never credible *down to the root*.

40 It is because each photograph always contains this imperious sign of my future death that each one, however attached it seems to be to the excited world of the living, challenges each of us, one by one, outside of any generality (but not outside of any transcendence). Further, photographs, except for an embarrassed ceremonial of a few boring evenings, are looked at when one is alone. I am uncomfortable during the private projection of a film (not enough of a public, not enough anonymity), but I need to be alone with the photographs I am looking at. Toward the end of the Middle Ages, certain believers substituted for collective reading or collective prayer an individual, under-the-breath prayer, interiorized and meditative (*devotio moderna*). Such, it seems to me, is the regime of *spectatio*. The reading of public photographs is always, at bottom, a private reading. This is obvious for old ("historical") photo-

III.

I was not there to see or touch her.
I did not prepare her casket or comb her hair.
These are my devotions, my burial rites:
I have run my hand along the limit of her.
I traced with love her cheek, her arm,
the thumb whose bend I know.
I limned the edge between us—
between her and the brink of this world.
I journeyed to her borders
and there I cut her free.

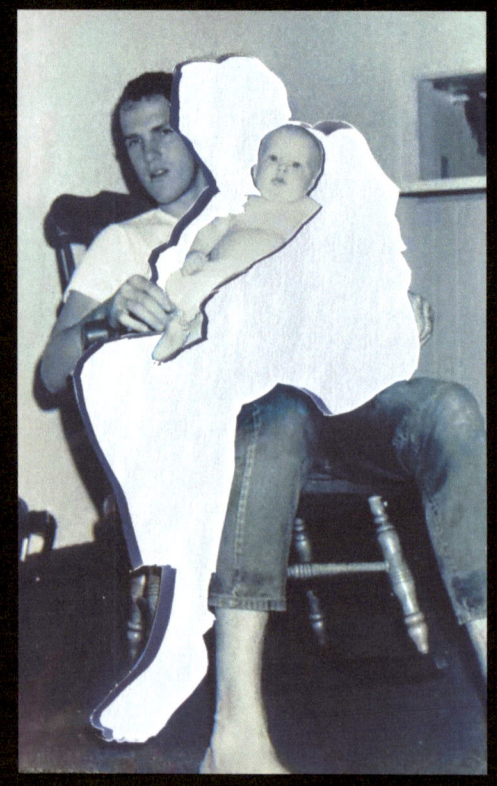

APRIL

I.

Late-March rain leaves LA glass-clear. From the bluffs above Playa del Rey, you can see all the way to my aunt's house at the foot of the San Gabriel Mountains, where my father and I are peeling clementines. We talk cautiously between bites of fruit, fearing to say too much lest each our separate sorrow meet the other's and compound to flood the desert.

Jacaranda, eucalyptus. Bougainvillea and oleander. Date palm, lemon, concrete, ice plant. The city where I was born.

I pass a day and a half with my father and aunt before checking into a downtown hotel for an academic conference. My dad is distracted. He spends much of our time together texting with a woman—an old friend, he says, with whom he has reconnected. I see him beaming happily at a photo of her he keeps on his phone. He buys trivial things in the shops on Colorado Boulevard. I assume that they're for her.

I understand this. I know how the impossible person pulsing in the palm of your hand can feel more alive than the family languishing in the shadow of your mourning. I am grateful to this woman for my father's respite from grief, for his stupid grin and whatever texted witticism has made him laugh unselfconsciously.

I understand, but I'm not prepared for this, and I withdraw from now and carry it away to feel about it later.

A flock of wild parrots settles in a nearby cypress. My father looks out from under the patio umbrella and mumbles in a weary voice, "I don't know what my life is supposed to be now."

II.

One of the more vivid details my mother passed on about her father's death was a discovery made during his autopsy. She said that they had found two hundred undissolved Seconal in his stomach. This element of his history made a strong impression on me. In my unscientific imagination, I pictured some crude anatomical bag slashed open, with grayish sludge spilling out, carrying a flotsam of white-and-yellow pills. I visualized the pathologist dutifully counting these macerated tablets and marking them down in his report. I never bothered to conjure up the rest of my grandfather's corpse: when I thought of him, I thought of this dim galaxy—this Milky Way of undigested pills.

Although my mother had referred to documents like the coroner's report and the final postcard my grandfather sent, I have never seen any records about his death. I have a wary sense that she kept them in a box in the recesses of her closet, and I have avoided encountering even the outside of this box. Now that they're both gone, it's time I see for myself what remains he left behind.

I ask my aunt if she thinks this box I've imagined actually exists and, if so, what my mother may have kept in it. She can't say with certainty. Instead, she brings out a box of her own. In it is my grandfather's death certificate. Suicide by acute barbiturate intoxication. No autopsy performed.

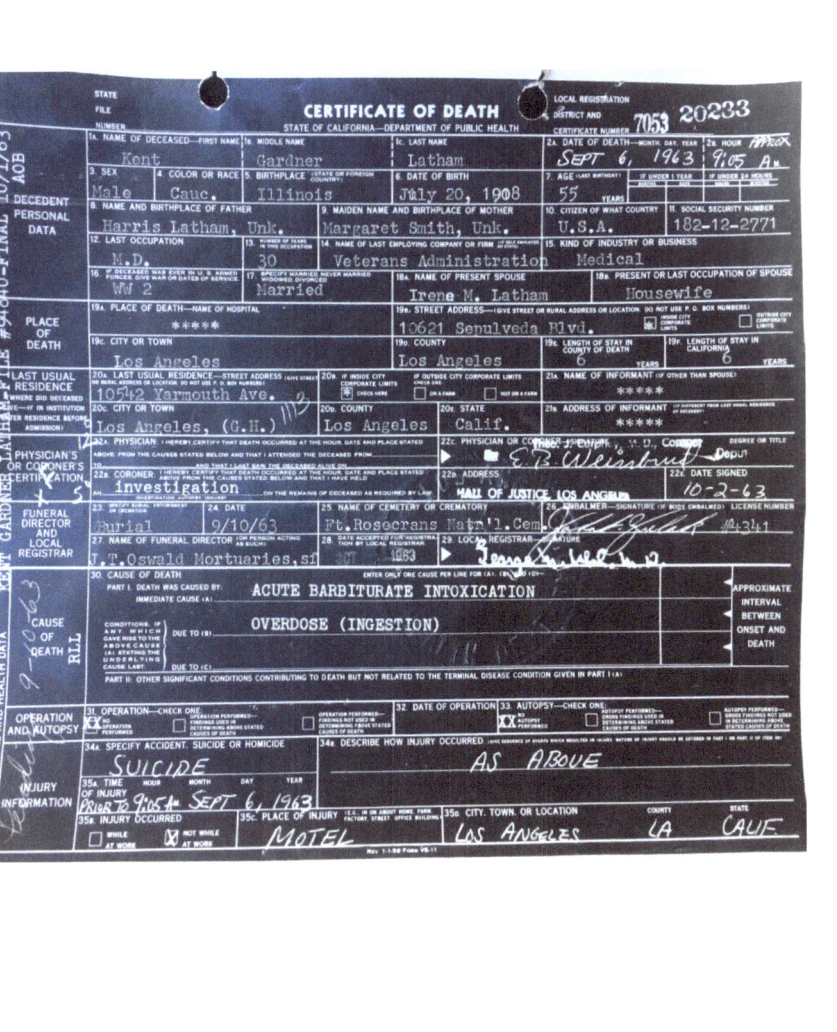

III.

In my aunt's box of history, I find a genealogy made by my grandfather, whose handwriting I'm seeing for the first time. He traces four generations—back to the Latham and Gardner ancestors who would give him his last and middle names. At the bottom of the long, folded page, he has written notes about several of his relatives. Roderick Gardner lived at Gardner Lake, Colchester, Connecticut. A bachelor on the old family property, Roy D. Gardner is "good for information." Hyde and Albert Gardner, my grandfather's great-uncles, "probably died young." And his uncle Seldon Gardner, number five in his neatly compiled legend, "died insane."

The *punctum*. The puncture. "That accident which pricks me (but also bruises me, is poignant to me.)"

5. Died insane

Where did he die insane? In an institution? At the family home on Gardner Lake? What did he die of, and how old was he when he died? How long had he been insane? What did "insane" mean when my grandfather wrote this in the 1930s?

He must have written it then, because the death of his older sister, the tragically named Desdemona, is not noted here. It is an event to come.

> 18. Desdemona Latham. Died young.

In this genealogy, the future is still open. My grandfather has not yet been sent to a field hospital in France where, helpless to put their bodies back together, he will watch a generation of numbered men die young. He has not yet returned from war so changed that he will eventually become "no longer able to work." He has not married my grandmother, Irene Murphy. He is not a father yet, not

> 19. Kent Gardner Latham. Suicide.

For now, he is poised on the edge of what will be—on the right margin of the paper, imminent.

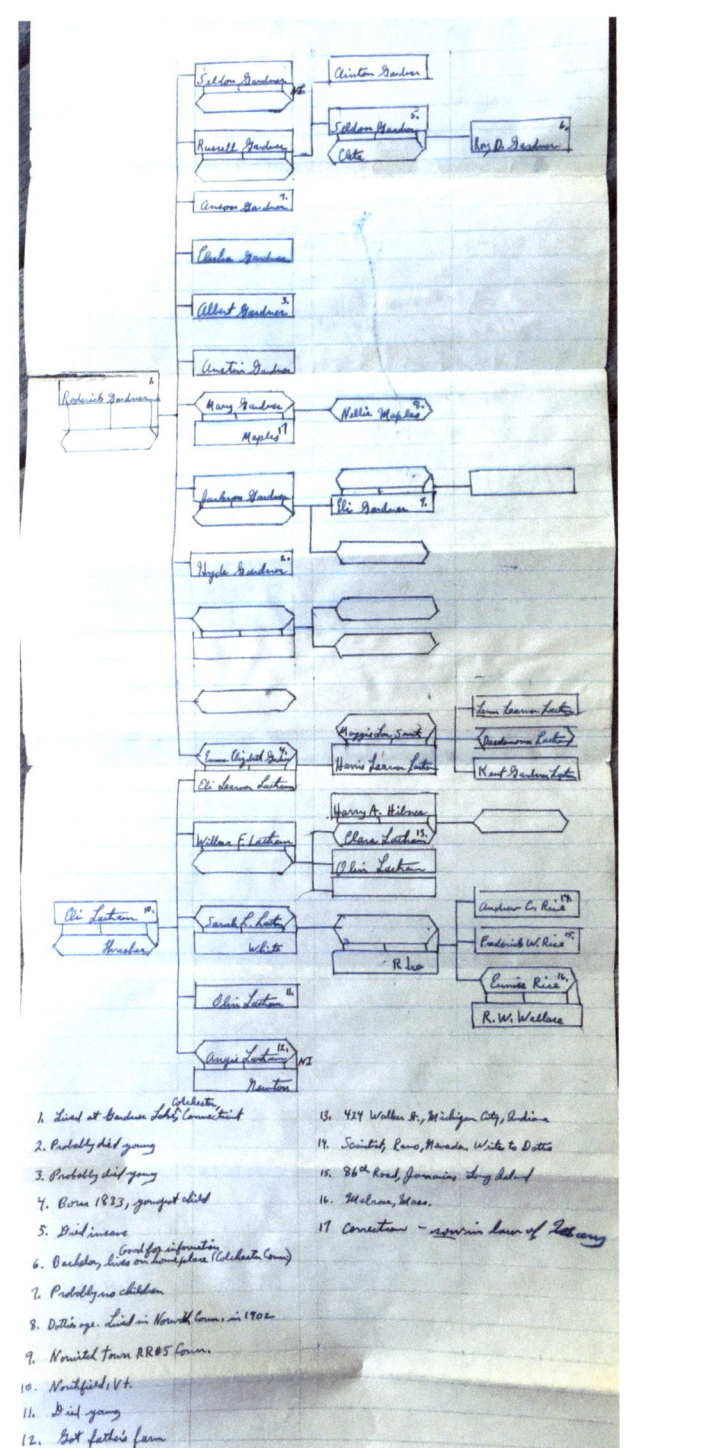

1. Lived at Gardner Lake, Colchester, Connecticut
2. Probably died young
3. Probably died young
4. Born 1833, youngest child
5. Died insane
6. Bachelor, lives on home place (Colchester Conn) Good for information
7. Probably no children
8. Dotties age. Lived in Norwich Conn. in 1902
9. Norwich town RR#5 Conn.
10. Northfield, Vt.
11. Died young
12. Got father's farm
13. 424 Walker St., Michigan City, Indiana
14. Scientist, Reno, Nevada. Write to Dottie
15. 86th Road, Jamaica, Long Island
16. Melrose, Mass.
17 Correction — now in favor of Bethany

IV.

I spend a weekend on the west side of Los Angeles with my college roommates, Niki and Arianna. It's good to be with them. They knew me when I was still becoming myself, and whatever I am now they will accept. Because I know this, I ask something of them without knowing why. I ask them to take me to Saint John's Hospital in Santa Monica, the hospital where I was born.

They drive me to the address we've looked up. It is Providence Saint John's Health Center now, and it has spread out to take up an entire city block along Santa Monica Boulevard. We pull over next to a building that looks new. I cannot have been born here. I have just turned forty-seven, and this building hasn't been here for forty-seven years. I get out of the car and walk down the street to look for the older part of the medical center. I will find out later that it was torn down and rebuilt after the Northridge earthquake. But I sense already that it doesn't matter what I'm looking at. I have not come for a building.

I know where I am. I am twenty blocks from the Pacific Ocean at the place where my mother brought me out of the water and into the land. It was here that I took my first breath of the magnolia air she had already taught me to want. Here I cried new-birthed tears at the calamity of it—at all I had lost in dividing from her and at all the loss that was to come.

This is my spring of trying not to cry in a street. Today, in this street, I don't put my sunglasses on or look for a closet or a crevice. I return to the car and hold my friends' hands, and I cry without shame or apology.

"What do you feel here?" Niki asks. Arianna gives me a squeeze.

> *Yes, I feel here.*
>
> *here she held me, I was her baby girl here.*
>
> *The first time she held me here.*

Was it also the last? When does ending begin?

At this crossroads here, the intersection of her life and mine.

There is no other time.

At this crossroads here

At this crossroads here

I feel the wondrous-terrible condition of making lives that die.

I feel my son.

Here. Baby, I am here.

I don't have any of these words. Instead, I fumble through all that I can say for now:
My mother is dead, and I am alive.

V.

I wake up in the early morning with an ache in my chest. This has been happening regularly, so I have googled it to make sure I'm not having a heart attack. The joints hurt where my ribs connect to my sternum. If I press on the cartilage, I can reproduce the pain.

My bones are far more prominent now than they were before I lost my appetite. I turn onto my back, which takes pressure off my chest, and I run my fingers over the ridges of my ribs where they meet my sternum. I am fascinated by the feel of them; I probe the sore cartilage. I wonder if this ache is what my mother felt when she began to develop arthritis. I didn't know that a ribcage had joints until she complained about the pain in her chest. There are things inside us that we don't know exist until they start to hurt.

My mother told a story many times that none of us believed. She said she had once seen a doctor about some physical ailment and that he had diagnosed her as unlovable. It was an absurd claim, and it irritated us that she retold it again and again as though it were remotely plausible. Later as an adult, I came to see this anecdote as an expression of something that felt very true for her: that the pain disabling her body was the story of her childhood in another form, as though an X-ray of her disfigured hands would disclose maternal rejection or a phlebotomy sample might return her father's death certificate. She carried their abandonment in the tissue and the bone.

The ache in my chest is not a secret or a story. It's just a thing that a body does, so close to the surface that I can touch it with my hand. This reassures me, and I lie in the dark prodding my ribs to remake this pain and this reassurance. My aging body is healthy. I do not believe myself unlovable. In these bones I carry my life, not hers.

ANOTHER TIME

ANOTHER TIME

In the myths of ancient Greece, the shades of the dead had to drink from the river Lethe before crossing into the Underworld. The waters of Lethe induced amnesia, allowing the dead to enter the afterlife free of the memory of life on earth.

I imagine my mother at the edge of this river. She knows what she is supposed to do; she has read all the books. But she does not take a drink as the other shades do. Instead, she dips in a toe. And then a foot. And then she wades into the current and begins to cross, her feet and legs, her torso and hands and arms and shoulders, her beautiful face—the face of my mother—vanishing forever in the swirling water.

On the far bank, something emerges that no human word can name. It is brilliant and fantastical. A form—or perhaps a formlessness—too abstract, too otherworldly for our minds of clay to imagine. It rises from the water and disappears into the future.

CREDITS

Unless otherwise noted, all artwork and scholarly extracts are the work of the author. In the interest of others' privacy, a few very minor details have been changed.

Front Matter

Etymology of "martyr": *The English Martyr from Reformation to Revolution* (Notre Dame, IN: University of Notre Dame Press, 2012), 29
Photo: My mother, Margaret Jean Leary (née Latham), Marine Corps Base Camp Lejeune, North Carolina, 1969

October

Script: Adapted from *The Spanish Tragedy* by Thomas Kyd, reproduced with permission of Dr. Chelsea Phillips
"Re-entry timeline": Wikipedia, "Space Shuttle *Columbia* Disaster," accessed November 2017 and May 2018; content no longer available; reproduced by permission of Wikipedia
"And this is the kingdom you bore me to": Sylvia Plath, "The Disquieting Muses"
Photo: My son, Halloween 2017; photo courtesy of Sondra Rosenberg
My family shooting off a rocket, Clark Air Base, Philippines, ca. 1980

November

"To be or not to be": William Shakespeare, *Hamlet*, act 3, scene 1

PowerPoint slide image: David Maisel, *History's Shadow* (GM1), 2010; © David Maisel; reproduced by permission of the artist

CWRU talk: Unpublished paper

"I cannot choose but weep": *Hamlet*, act 4, scene 5

Photo: My mother's burial service, Miramar National Cemetery, San Diego, California, November 21, 2017

Another Time

Photo: My maternal grandfather, Kent Gardner Latham, ca. 1938

"Day now, night now, at head, side, feet": Sylvia Plath, "The Disquieting Muses"

Photo: My maternal grandmother, Irene Latham, ca. 1955

December

"A Valediction: Forbidding Mourning": John Donne

"XII. Graves We Filled before the Fire": Gabrielle Calvocoressi, "Circus Fire, 1944," in *The Last Time I Saw Amelia Earhart* (New York: Persea Books, 2005); © Gabrielle Calvocoressi; reproduced by permission of the poet; reprinted by permission of Persea Books, Inc. (New York)

Prince Harry and Henry IV: Shakespeare, *The Second Part of Henry IV*, act 4, scene 3

"Trouble enough can come": Margaret Jean Leary (née Latham), date unknown (prior to 1969)

Another Time

"This is not a story to pass on": Toni Morrison, *Beloved* (New York: Plume Books, 1988), 275

CREDITS

January

Richard of Gloucester (later Richard III): adapted from Shakespeare, *The Third Part of Henry VI*, act 5, scene 6
Photo: My boots, January 2018
Photo: My father, Christmas Day, 2017
Andy Warhol Foundation Electric Chair Leather Bucket Bag, https://shop.nordstrom.com/s/calvin-klein-205w39nyc-x-andy-warhol-foundation-electricchair-leather-bucket-bag/4862434; accessed February and May 2018
"By reproducing a photograph . . .": from a draft of "The King Machine: Reproducing Sovereignty in *3 Henry VI*," subsequently published in *How to Do Things with Dead People: History, Technology, and Temporality from Shakespeare to Warhol* (Ithaca, NY: Cornell University Press, 2022), chap. 4
Photo: My mother's headstone, Miramar National Cemetery, San Diego, California, January 2018

Another Time

Photo: The exhumation of Richard III, Leicester, England, November 2011; © Darlow Smithson Productions, UK
Photo: My mother's second-grade class, Elmhurst, Illinois, 1956
Index: *The English Martyr*, 320
"The legend of Saint Apollonia . . .": "Stigma and Stigmata: Medieval Hagiography and Michael Landy's *Saints Alive*," *Word & Image* 32, no. 3 (2016): 275–93, quotation on 287
Photo: My mother dressed for her first communion, 1956
"But the function of martyr literature . . .": *English Martyr*, 250–51

February

Photo: Andy Warhol, *Marilyn x 100* (1962), Cleveland Museum of Art, February 2, 2018; © 2023 The Andy Warhol Foundation for the Visual Arts, Inc. / Licensed by Artists Rights Society (ARS), New York; Rights of Publicity and Persona Rights: The Estate of Marilyn Monroe LLC, marilynmonroe.com

Photo: Tattoo inspired by Shaun Tan, *The Arrival* (New York: Arthur A. Levine, 2007)

"'Farewell, Kafka Tamura' . . .": Haruki Murakami, *Kafka on the Shore*, translated by Philip Gabriel, 582; translation copyright © 2005 by Haruki Murakami; used by permission of Alfred A. Knopf, an imprint of the Knopf Doubleday Publishing Group, a division of Penguin Random House LLC; all rights reserved

Photos: Clementines, February and March 2018

"The Exchange": Margaret Leary, January 31, 1993

What in Me Is Dark

"what in me is dark": John Milton, *Paradise Lost*, 1.22

"The mother's body is typically the child's first food": Sondra Rosenberg, *The Art of Recovery* (unpublished manuscript in progress)

March

"our lives like barns . . .": Gabrielle Calvocoressi, "From the Adult Drive-in," IX, *The Last Time I Saw Amelia Earhart* (New York: Persea Books, 2005); © Gabrielle Calvocoressi; reproduced by permission of the poet; reprinted by permission of Persea Books, Inc. (New York)

Photos: My house after Winter Storm Riley, March 2, 2018

Photo: My son while an inpatient at Children's Hospital of Philadelphia, August 2012

Another Time

Photo: My father's kindergarten class, Northridge, California, 1954
Photo: My father, Rapid City, North Dakota, ca. 1953
Studium and *punctum*: Roland Barthes, *Camera Lucida: Reflections on Photography,* trans. Richard Howard (New York: Hill and Wang, 1980), 26–27, 96–97
Family photos, 1969–2012

April

California Certificate of Death for Kent Gardner Latham, d. September 6, 1963
Genealogy written by my maternal grandfather, Kent Gardner Latham, ca. 1935
Photo: My grandfather and his siblings, ca. 1911
Photo: Saint John's Hospital, Santa Monica, California, ca. 1970; source unknown

Another Time

Photo: My mother, ca. 1969

ACKNOWLEDGMENTS

My abiding gratitude—

To the artists and writers who are cited in these pages, especially Gabrielle Calvocoressi and David Maisel.

To the friends and colleagues who have supported me in this work: Chelsea Biondolillo, Tom Cartelli, Chris Daley, Mark Dean, Tsering Wangmo Dhompa, Alan Drew, Joseph Drury, Andrew Hartley, Heather Hicks, Shawn Kairschner, Zachary Lesser, Mary Mullen, Brett Garcia Myhren, Adrienne Perry, Kristen Poole, Michael Risch, Sondra Rosenberg, and Lisa Sewell.

To Tessie Prakas, Colleen Rosenfeld, and the scholars of The Renaissance Project.

To Charlie Gill for assistance with images.

To Brendan Maher and Hannah Kahn for research assistance.

To the Villanova University Publication Subvention Program and the College of Arts and Sciences for support for image reproduction.

To Tom Lay and my readers and production team at Fordham University Press.

To Taije Silverman for many things, but especially for "I am determined to give what is mine to give."

To this book's patron saint, the luminous and incomparable Wendy Beth Hyman.

To my family, without whose generosity, love, courage, and grace this book would not have been possible.

www.ingramcontent.com/pod-product-compliance
Lightning Source LLC
Chambersburg PA
CBHW041227070526
44584CB00006B/323